The Community's COLLEGE

Indicators *of* Engagement *at* Two-Year Institutions

Edward Zlotkowski
Donna Killian Duffy
Robert Franco
Sherril B. Gelmon
Katrina H. Norvell
Jennifer Meeropol
Steven Jones

Table of Contents

Acknowledgements

We would like to thank our colleagues at Campus Compact for their assistance in various aspects of this project. Elizabeth Hollander contributed to the creation of the original indicators of engagement and provided valuable guidance throughout this project. John Saltmarsh, another author of the original indicators, provided valuable insight, direction, and feedback throughout the project. Karen Partridge served as volume editor and helped ensure the consistency and integrity of the text. Jan Torres and William Beaird guided the original proposal that funded the project and provided valuable early guidance.

State Compact Directors identified and recommended model community colleges in their states, encouraged their members to participate in this project, made recommendation about project design and implementation, and, in some cases, participated in the site visits.

Gail Robinson, Coordinator of Service-Learning at the American Association of Community Colleges (AACC), was instrumental in designing the survey of engagement at community colleges and helped guide the initial development of the project. Along with Jeffrey Mills, she also provided technical support for the web survey. We are grateful to AACC, Gail, and Jeffrey for their assistance.

Student interns Regina Pei and Deborah List assisted with project details and provided administrative support. Allyse Heartwell served as a writing intern, helping to draft initial language for the monograph and assisting with fact-checking and tracking down documentation and additional information.

We are grateful to the Carnegie Corporation of New York for their generous support of this project and to our program officer, Cynthia Gibson, for her insights and recommendations.

Atlantic Philanthropies provided funding for a meeting to discuss civic and community engagement at community colleges. This meeting provided valuable insight that helped guide the early course of the project.

Finally, we wish to thank the individuals from community colleges who completed the survey, participated in telephone interviews, hosted the site visits, spoke with our scholars, and collected and submitted their documents for our use. Many individuals took time out of their busy lives to share their stories, successes, and challenges with us. This book would not have been possible without their generosity and commitment. We thank them for both.

Introduction

> *"An individual has not started living until he can rise above the narrow confines of his individualistic concerns to the broader concerns of all humanity."*
>
> DR. MARTIN LUTHER KING, JR.

Higher Education and American Democracy

In 21st century America, the challenge of bringing new life to American democracy may be the most important issue facing the nation. A multi-decade decline in civic participation has led many eminent sociologists, political scientists, and government and nonprofit leaders to sound an alarm. These diverse voices focus on different aspects of civic life, but the overall concern is the same: in the words of the much-cited Nunn/Bennett Commission report, we have become a "nation of spectators" who have distanced ourselves from our civic responsibilities (National Commission on Civic Renewal, 1998).

Of particular concern is the lack of democratic participation among young Americans, a group shown time and again to be alienated from government and deeply cynical about the political system (Sax et al., 1999; The Institute of Politics, 2000; National Association of Secretaries of State, 1999; The Mellman Group, 2000). Since it has long been a goal of American higher education—and particularly of America's community colleges—to develop well-informed, critically thinking citizens, the challenge now is to harness the power of higher education to educate the next generation of active citizens.

Frequently cited studies about today's college generation emphasize the civic deficits of students as citizens. Students in these studies express little faith in institutions, little knowledge of their own democratic structures, and little interest in keeping up with public affairs. They are turned off by the dominance of big money in politics and have little trust in politicians. They vote in low numbers (although much higher on a percentage basis than their non-college peers) and seem to feel little sense of agency in affecting public policy.

On the other hand, today's students are involved in public and community service to a greater extent than has been true for decades. Here they are neither passive nor disengaged. They have an active interest in global equity and in local community development. They have an extraordinary sensitivity to multicultural issues and the importance of learning to work with those who are different from themselves. They want to make a difference; they simply prefer to do so through individual service.

Higher education institutions are well positioned to harness this energy and direct it in ways that can benefit their communities and deepen their students' education at the same time. Yet colleges and universities are subject to the same forces that are challenging all civic institutions. Rapid technological change, globalization, demand for workforce training, and increasing pressure to raise funds from the private sector all distract higher education's attention from the civic aspect of its mission.

Higher education institutions are well positioned to harness this energy and direct it in ways that can benefit their communities and deepen their students' education at the same time.

Despite these distractions, academic leaders have shown themselves to be increasingly interested in reasserting the civic purpose of their institutions. This reassertion of civic mission is evidenced by the 535 college and university presidents who have signed the *Presidents' Declaration on the Civic Responsibility of Higher Education* (Campus Compact, 1999, 2004). Leadership like this has, in turn, helped generate major community and civic initiatives at higher education institutions across the country. Faculty, deans, department chairs, and chief academic officers, supported by their presidents, campus staff, and national disciplinary associations, have created service-learning programs as well as other forms of civic engagement such as substantive campus/community partnerships, public dialogues, diversity agendas, and new ways to recognize and reward the scholarship of engagement.

Among all engagement efforts, service-learning is probably the most widespread and best known strategy aimed at equipping students with the knowledge and skills needed for democratic citizenship. Service-learning links academic with community learning by incorporating relevant community work into a college course. In addition to deepening students' content knowledge, service-learning has proved effective in exposing students to "the other America," deepening their multicultural understanding and tolerance, increasing their understanding of community dynamics, and improving their ability to relate theory to practice. At its best, it helps students link their academic learning to real-world work environments, to the conditions they experience in the community, and to larger questions of social equity. For this reason, service-learning is an important feature of campus-based civic engagement. The colleges discussed in this monograph use service-learning, community service, student activism, community based research, and other civic engagement strategies to create engaged campuses.

Campus Compact and the Growth of Campus Engagement

In 1985, the presidents of Brown, Georgetown, and Stanford Universities, along with the president of the Education Commission of the States, joined together to form Campus Compact, a coalition of college and university presidents committed to fulfilling the civic purposes of higher education. To support this civic mission, Campus Compact promotes service initiatives that develop students' citizenship skills, helps campuses forge effective community partnerships, and provides resources and practical guidance for faculty seeking to integrate civic engagement into their teaching and research. Member presidents believe that by creating a supportive campus environment for engagement in community service, colleges and universities can best prepare their students to be active, committed, and informed citizens and community leaders.

Campus Compact's growth in membership is one strong indicator of higher education's renewed commitment to its civic mission. Membership has grown by more than 30% in the past four years to more than 920 member institutions. Furthermore, the rich diversity of Campus Compact's membership reflects the civic commitment of institutions across the spectrum of higher education: 52% of member campuses are public and 48% are private, encompassing women's, faith-based, historically black, Hispanic-serving, and tribal institutions. Nearly 25% of its members are community or two-year colleges.

Creating an Engaged Campus

As campus-based civic engagement has grown, finding ways to measure, assess, expand, and improve engagement efforts has become an increasingly important priority. To meet this need, Campus Compact developed the Civic Engagement/ Service-Learning Pyramid, a schematic representation of the developmental levels of engagement activities on campuses.

The pyramid has three levels: Introductory, Intermediate, and Advanced. Each level has a set of characteristics appropriate for the constituency involved. Thus, the full picture of each level is quite complex, defined as it is by the roles and needs of multiple constituencies that act both as stakeholders and as agents of institutional change: presidents, chief academic officers, faculty, community service directors, community partners, and students. The advanced level represents the fully "engaged campus"—an institution whose mission, purpose, and support structures are aligned with the needs of the local community. The engaged campus has been described as having "an integrated approach to fostering students' citizenship skills through both educational and co-curricular programs and activities, and conscious modeling of good institutional citizenship through external partnerships and activities" (Thomas, 2000, p. 66). This level also reflects full acceptance of that larger sense of institutional alignment Ernest Boyer identified as "the scholarship of engagement"; namely, scholarship that "connect[s] the rich resources of the university to our most pressing social, civic, and ethical problems" (Boyer, 1996a).

The three levels of the pyramid reflect the journey of an institution in achieving a richer and deeper commitment to community outreach, service-learning, civic engagement, and the scholarship of engagement. At each level, a number of key indicators serve to mark the institution's progress (Figure 1).

Figure 1: **Civic Engagement/Service-Learning Pyramid**

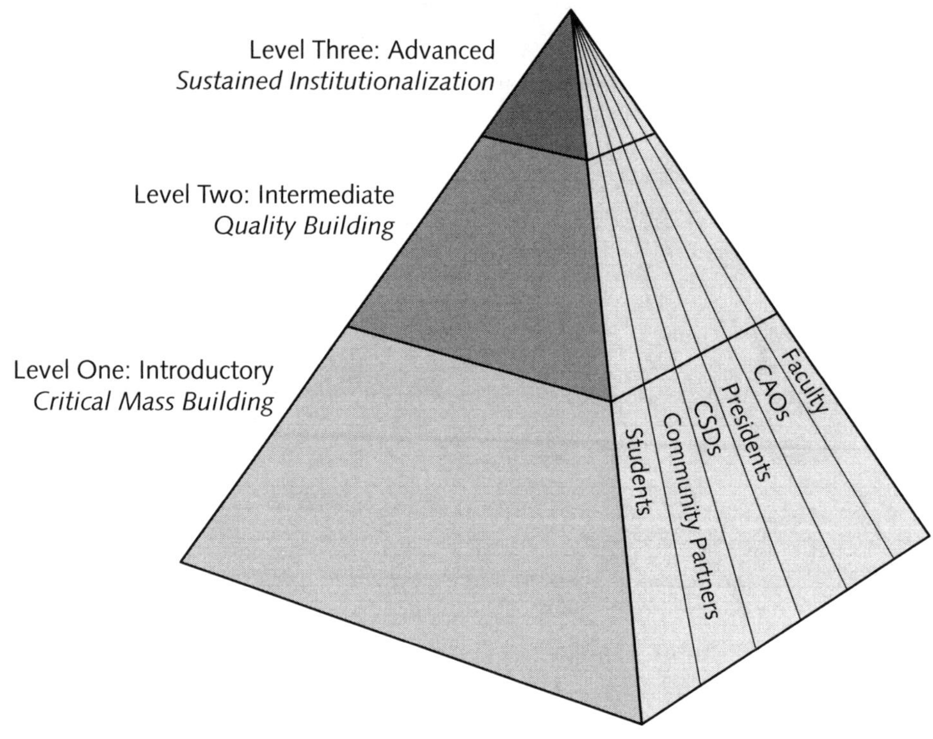

The Indicators of Engagement

The indicators should not be regarded as prescriptive; their value lies primarily in the possibilities they suggest.

The pyramid in Figure 1 lists 13 indicators of engagement that correspond to the three levels of engagement. The indicators were developed by Campus Compact executive director Elizabeth Hollander, project director John Saltmarsh, and senior faculty fellow Edward Zlotkowski (Hollander and Saltmarsh, 2000; Hollander, Saltmarsh, and Zlotkowski, 2001) to capture the various approaches to engagement they observed at institutions across the country. The indicators are designed to help campuses both assess their current level of engagement and create strategies to deepen their work. The developers of the indicators used a broad range of criteria, recognizing that institutions utilize the approaches to engagement best suited to their particular culture and priorities. It is unlikely that any one campus, however engaged, will exhibit all of the indicators to an equal extent. For this reason, the indicators should not be regarded as prescriptive; their value lies primarily in the possibilities they suggest.

CAMPUS CHARACTERISTICS AT EACH LEVEL OF ENGAGEMENT

Institutional Characteristics of Level One: Introductory Practice

Level One is the *Critical Mass Building* stage (Furco, 2001). At this stage campuses are beginning to recognize the value of community engagement and are building a campus-wide constituency for the effort.

Campuses at the introductory stage are building awareness among faculty, students, and community partners; debating, discussing, and clarifying the meaning of service-learning and civic engagement in the context of institutional mission; and considering the need for institutional support.

Institutional Characteristics of Level Two: Intermediate Practice

Level Two is the *Quality Building* stage. At this stage campuses focus on ensuring the development of "quality" engagement activities; the quality of activities begins to supercede their quantity.

Intermediate campuses have a critical mass of faculty involvement and support, multiple student opportunities for service and civic engagement, sound community partnerships, and a funded infrastructure on campus.

Institutional Characteristics of Level Three: Advanced Practice

Level Three is the *Sustained Institutionalization* stage. It is at this stage that a campus has fully integrated service-learning and civic engagement into the fabric of the institution, creating an "engaged campus" characterized by recognizable institutional activities, policies, and structures.

Institutionalization is evident in the alignment of civic engagement with institutional mission. Faculty have incentives and rewards for implementing an engaged pedagogy. Students exercise high levels of leadership and are also rewarded for engagement. The community is a partner in the educational process, and the institution regularly assesses and plans its ongoing engagement efforts.

The 13 indicators of engagement are defined as follows:

1) **Mission and purpose** explicitly articulate a commitment to the public purposes of higher education.

2) **Administrative and academic leadership** (president, trustees, provost) is in the forefront of institutional transformation that supports civic engagement.

3) **Disciplines, departments, and interdisciplinary work** have incorporated community-based education, allowing it to penetrate across disciplines and reach the institution's academic core.

4) **Pedagogy and epistemology** incorporate a community-based, public problem-solving approach to teaching and learning.

5) **Faculty development** opportunities are available for faculty to retool their teaching and redesign their curricula to incorporate community-based activities and reflection on those activities within the context of the course.

6) **Faculty roles and rewards,** including promotion and tenure guidelines and review, reflect a reconsideration of scholarship that embraces a scholarship of engagement.

7) **Enabling mechanisms** are present in the form of visible and easily accessible structures (e.g., centers, offices) on campus to assist faculty with community-based teaching and to broker community partnerships.

8) **Internal resource allocation** is adequate for establishing, enhancing, and deepening community-based work on campus—for faculty, students, and programs that involve community partners.

9) **Community voice** deepens the role of community partners in contributing to community-based education and shaping outcomes that benefit the community.

10) **External resource allocation** is made available for community partners to create richer learning environments for students and for community-building efforts in local neighborhoods.

11) **Integrated and complementary engagement activities** weave together student service, service-learning, and other community engagement activities on campus.

12) **Forums for fostering public dialogue** are created that include multiple stakeholders in public problem-solving.

13) **Student voice** is cultivated in a way that recognizes students as key partners in their own education and civic development and supports their efforts to act on issues important to themselves and their peers.

Campus Compact's Indicators of Engagement Project (IOEP)

Colleges are eager for reliable information about how to achieve an engaged campus. This is evident from Campus Compact's annual member survey; in 2003, respondents identified Campus Compact's most valuable services as providing resource materials (97%) and identifying model programs (93%). National leaders have also called upon Campus Compact to provide more information on campus engagement practices, seeing such information as an essential tool in advancing national policy. However, several barriers exist to gathering such information. One is the need for a conceptual framework that respects the tremendous diversity of American colleges and universities. Another is the difficulty of capturing all of the relevant practices on a campus and determining whether, in fact, they represent "models" of engagement. Finally, there is the challenge of documenting practice with enough specificity to be truly useful.

Campus Compact has experimented with a number of ways to develop model program information, including self-reports of best practice, small grants to campuses to document their practice, and self-evaluation grants made available by state Campus Compact offices. Each strategy has produced some useful information, but none has been organized in a way that can powerfully effect change.

In May 2002 Campus Compact received a grant from the Carnegie Corporation of New York to combine documentation and dissemination of best practices of civic engagement with an organizing effort to help campuses achieve broader institutionalization of that engagement. In structuring the resulting Indicators of Engagement Project (IOEP), Campus Compact realized that higher education's segmentation based on institutional type, region, and peer group—as well as the significance of an institution's place, history, and local identity—limits the usefulness of any single "engaged campus" model across higher education. Instead, campuses need a *variety* of exemplary practices that they can use to create civic engagement strategies appropriate to their particular type of institution and specific community needs.

Hence, the IOEP seeks to identify, document, and disseminate best practices of civic engagement at different types of institutions. Each year of the grant focuses on a different institutional type: community colleges in year one and minority-serving institutions (including Historically Black colleges and universities, Tribal colleges, and Hispanic-serving institutions) in year two. In all cases, the project seeks to capture the diversity within each institutional type by including broad representation based on geography, setting (e.g., urban, rural, suburban), size, and other characteristics. The 13 indicators of engagement are the organizing framework for this documentation effort.

Community Colleges and the IOEP

Campus Compact staff chose to focus the first year of the project on engagement at community colleges for several reasons. First and most important, these colleges' natural connection to their communities makes them uniquely suited to develop engagement strategies. Second, despite both this natural affinity for engagement and the many exemplary practices community colleges have developed, this sector has been generally underserved and understudied in the literature on civic engagement. Campus Compact believed that an initial focus on community colleges would serve both community colleges and the larger field—which has much to learn from community colleges—while at the same time providing an excellent opportunity to test the indicators of engagement at institutions whose mission and circumstances often make engagement an institutional priority.

Community colleges' natural connection to their communities makes them uniquely suited to develop engagement strategies.

Changing demographics also influenced the decision to focus the first year of the project on community colleges. According to recent studies, nearly half of all undergraduates are enrolled at community colleges. Furthermore, the majority of first-generation, immigrant, and minority students enrolled in postsecondary education attend community college. Community colleges thus serve many of the fastest-growing college populations. As Margaret A. Miller has noted, "Imagine a series of portraits in which a young, white male face on the left morphs into a middle-aged, brown, female face on the right. That, in short, is the changing face of higher education in the United States today" (2003, p. 4). Clearly, any successful expansion of civic engagement in higher education must include community colleges.

The relevance of civic engagement to community colleges is clearly illustrated in the exemplary work of the two-year institutions highlighted in this monograph. Project staff used a variety of research tools to identify these schools, including a web-based survey to identify promising practices, telephone interviews to determine exemplary practices, site visits to thirteen selected institutions, and in-depth telephone interviews with an additional six schools. Site visitors and interviewers used protocols developed for assessment across multiple sites and researchers, including standardized interview protocols for each indicator of engagement and stakeholder group. (Additional information about the research methodology is included in Appendix I.) Examples and quotations included in this monograph were collected during telephone interviews with and site visits to participating schools.

COMMUNITY COLLEGES INCLUDED IN THIS PROJECT

Albuquerque Technical Vocational Institute (NM)	Malcolm X College (IL)
Anne Arundel Community College (MD)	Miami Dade College (FL)
Brevard Community College (FL)	Middlesex Community College (MA)
Chandler-Gilbert Community College (AZ)	Mount Wachusett Community College (MA)
College of Lake County (IL)	Portland Community College (OR)
Collin County Community College District (TX)	Raritan Valley Community College (NJ)
Hocking College (OH)	Southern Maine Community College (ME)
Johnson County Community College (KS)	Virginia Highlands Community College (VA)
Kapi'olani Community College (HI)	Yakima Valley Community College (WA)
Kirtland Community College (MI)	

About This Volume

The present volume seeks to address a variety of constituencies: faculty, students, administrators, and others in the higher education community interested in civic engagement, as well as community leaders seeking to partner with community colleges. Campus Compact hopes the volume's documentation will be sufficiently persuasive to make a strong case for continued and even increased support for local, state, and national policies and programs that support civic engagement at community colleges.

The text is divided into seven chapters. The first chapter, **Community Colleges and the Civic Engagement Movement,** provides context for the project findings. This framing chapter explores the history of community colleges in the United States and locates the current project within the context of earlier initiatives to increase engagement at community colleges.

For the project findings, rather than deal with each indicator separately, we have grouped them into five thematic clusters. This approach minimizes repetition while allowing us to create larger units of coherence within which to explore the engaged campus. The findings highlight the work of community colleges that excel in certain aspects of engagement, as measured by the indicators. These exemplary practices serve as models of engagement for all of higher education.

The chapter on **Institutional Culture** acknowledges that although all community colleges are connected with their communities, a wide spectrum of possibilities exists for understanding and acting on this connection. This chapter examines those indicators that help establish a culture of engagement that demonstrably affects the ways in which faculty, students, and community partners experience the goals and priorities of the college. These indicators include *mission and purpose* and *administrative and academic leadership.*

Curriculum and Pedagogy focuses on one of the most important lessons of the last decade: civic engagement must be rooted in the core work of the college if it is to be effectively spread throughout the institution. Since the core work of the college is teaching and learning, civic engagement must be linked directly to the curriculum. This chapter looks at those indicators—*disciplines, departments, and interdisciplinary work* and *pedagogy and epistemology*—that measure the degree to which community-related work has become part of the institution's teaching and learning activities.

Civic engagement must be rooted in the core work of the college if it is to be effectively spread throughout the institution.

Closely related to curricular issues are issues of faculty identity. If faculty feel neither prepared nor rewarded for their engaged work, the curricular connection cannot long survive. **Faculty Roles and Rewards** examines faculty culture and the two indicators, *faculty development* and *faculty roles and rewards,* that suggest faculty are getting the support they need to undertake the task of linking the curriculum to the community.

However, successful engagement depends not only on institutional culture and faculty self-understanding; it also depends—rather directly—on the concrete and specific resources the college is willing to commit to support civic engagement. Such a commitment must be deep enough to survive the pressures of competing priorities and difficult economic times. **Mechanisms and Resources** looks at indicators that determine whether community concerns can hold their own in the face of decisions regarding the bottom line. It also explores the ways in which students themselves are empowered to support the engagement process. The indicators included here are *internal resource allocation, enabling mechanisms, integrated and complementary engagement activities,* and *student voice.*

Finally, we turn to the off-campus community itself. Civic engagement means more than successful "outreach" in the traditional sense. It also presupposes an important shift in the way in which the higher education institution regards the surrounding community. No longer does the college act on its own, however benign its intentions. Instead, it recognizes the community as an equal partner, fully entitled to participate in all matters affecting the two. **Community-Campus Exchange** explores indicators that measure the community role in the engagement process: *external resource allocation, community voice,* and *forums for fostering public dialogue.*

The **Conclusion** focuses on the implications of the project's findings. Reviewing those findings in the context of the civic engagement movement as a whole, the chapter explores the importance of fully recognizing—and supporting—the community college role in creating the next generation of active citizens. It also raises questions and identifies issues still needing to be explored.

Finally, the appendices include a discussion of **project methodology,** which addresses the research approach utilized here and evaluates key decisions and outcomes as well as the project findings; a **self-assessment guide** for using the indicators to gauge and further advance engagement on your campus; and a list of **key contacts** at the colleges studied for this project.

Biographical Notes on Volume Contributors

Dr. Edward Zlotkowski is the senior scholar for the Indicators of Engagement Project. Dr. Zlotkowski is a professor of English at Bentley College in Waltham, MA, where he founded the Bentley College Service-Learning Center in 1990. As the senior faculty fellow at Campus Compact, he directs the organization's initiative on service-learning in the disciplines. He is the editor of *Successful Service-Learning Programs* (Anker Publishing, 1998) and *Service-Learning and the First-Year Experience* (Resource Center for the First-Year Experience and Students in Transition, University of South Carolina, 2002). He also serves as series editor of the American Association for Higher Education (AAHE)/Campus Compact series of books on service-learning in the disciplines. Dr. Zlotkowski drafted the five chapters in this volume that discuss project findings and the conclusion, and served as monograph editor.

Dr. Donna Killian Duffy is a Campus Compact community college engaged scholar for the first year of the IOEP. Dr. Duffy, a professor of psychology at Middlesex Community College in Lowell, MA, is the coeditor of *With Service in Mind,* a monograph on service-learning in psychology (AAHE, 1998). She received the Thomas Ehrlich Faculty Award for Service-Learning in 1999 for her work connecting service in the community to student learning in the classroom and has presented and written extensively on the topic. She has worked with the American Psychological

Association to create its website on service-learning and civic engagement and to introduce service-learning into programs for preparing future faculty. Dr. Duffy conducted the initial review of all documentation provided by the colleges, which established a foundation for the findings chapters of this book.

Dr. Robert Franco is also a community college engaged scholar for the first year of the IOEP. Dr. Franco is director of planning and grants and professor of anthropology at Kapi'olani Community College in Honolulu, HI, and is a Service-Learning National Trainer for the National Youth Leadership Council Learn and Serve Exchange. A recognized expert on community colleges in the United States, Dr. Franco has traveled to more than 100 community colleges across the nation, often as a consulting expert on how best to initiate and institutionalize service-learning and civic engagement programs. He has also presented and written extensively on the topic. Dr. Franco wrote the first chapter on the community college context and parts of the conclusion for this study.

Dr. Sherril Gelmon, professor of public health at Portland State University (Portland, OR), is Campus Compact's engaged scholar on assessment and the evaluation director for the IOEP. Dr. Gelmon has extensive experience in designing and evaluating multi-institutional and interdisciplinary projects related to civic engagement and service-learning. She is the lead author of a seminal assessment guide, *Assessing Service-Learning and Civic Engagement: Principles and Techniques* (Campus Compact, 2001), and a co-author of *The Engaged Department Toolkit* (Campus Compact, 2003). As the engaged scholar on assessment, she has provided evaluative consultation to Campus Compact's work on civic engagement in the disciplines. Dr. Gelmon was the primary author on the methodology discussion in Appendix I.

Katrina Norvell assists Dr. Gelmon with the project evaluation. Ms. Norvell is a doctoral student in the public administration and policy program at Portland State University. She assists in program evaluation of projects on community-based nursing education and nonprofit leadership development in minority communities. Ms. Norvell assisted Dr. Gelmon in writing the methodology discussion.

Jennifer Meeropol is the project coordinator for the Indicators of Engagement Project. Ms. Meeropol has worked in higher education administration at Harvard Medical School and at Brown University. She has also served as Campus Compact's resource coordinator. As project coordinator for the IOEP, Ms. Meeropol oversees the daily management of all project activities and coordinates the efforts of internal and external project staff. Ms. Meeropol wrote the Introduction to the monograph, drafted the sidebars in the five findings chapters, and managed the process of writing the monograph.

Dr. Steven Jones, project associate for the Integrating Service with Academic Studies (ISAS) project at Campus Compact, is a member of the IOEP team. Prior to joining Campus Compact, Dr. Jones was associate professor of political science at the University of Charleston, where he also served as director of the Robert C. Byrd

Institute for Government Policy. In addition to his work with the ISAS project, he coordinates Campus Compact's national outreach and support services for community colleges. Dr. Jones conducted telephone interviews, analyzed data, and helped draft the conclusion of this volume.

Community Colleges and the Civic Engagement Movement

> *"I believe the community college is the most dynamic contribution America has ever made to higher learning."*
>
> EVAN S. DOBELLE, PRESIDENT
> UNIVERSITY OF HAWAII SYSTEM

America's Democracy Colleges: A Century of Evolution

America's community colleges began with a civic ideal: they were created in the early 1900s to democratize both American higher education and the students who came through their doors. Early proponents of what were then called junior colleges referred to them as America's "democracy colleges," giving millions of worthy students who would otherwise have been excluded a chance to attend higher education. Community colleges have always been institutions that stand for equal opportunity; as such, they have been a key component of America's democratic infrastructure. (For further discussion see Franco, 2000, 2002a, 2002b.)

Although community colleges have retained this purpose throughout their 100-year history, the form their civic mission takes has proved highly mutable. Throughout the first quarter of the 20th century, junior colleges emphasized successful university transfer, together with engagement in the civic and social issues of the communities they served. By the mid-1920s, a counter-movement stressing the role of the junior college as a provider of terminal and vocational education had began to gather momentum (Brint and Karabel, 1991).

In the 1940s, as the United States began to emerge from World War II, the focus on community issues and access sharpened. In the aftermath of the war, the Truman Commission defined a specific community-engaged mission for America's community colleges:

> The Community College seeks to become a center of learning for the entire community with or without the restrictions that surround formal course work in traditional institutions of higher education. It gears its programs and services to the needs and wishes of the people it serves (President's Commission on Higher Education, 1947).

The Truman Commission called for public education to be "made available, tuition-free, to all Americans able and willing to receive it, regardless of race, creed, color, sex, or economic and social status" (Gleazer, 1994). Even before the war actually ended, with millions of former service personnel returning from the European and Pacific theaters, pressure to extend educational opportunities resulted in the passage of the G.I. Bill in 1944. This, in turn, led to soaring enrollments in community colleges through 1948.

Community colleges were not just *in*, they were *of*, *by*, and *for* the people in their surrounding area.

In the second half of the 20th century, community colleges became an increasingly important feature of America's cultural geography. Many of them emerged to meet the educational needs of residents in established cities and towns. Others sprang up as America's suburban dream became a reality and as a vast rural America became integrated into the world's most accessible higher education system (Association of American Colleges and Universities, 2002). By the 1990s, most Americans had a community college within commuting distance of their homes or jobs. These colleges reflected the diversity of the neighborhoods they served; like the local K-12 schools that prepared their students, community colleges were not just *in,* they were *of, by,* and *for* the people in their surrounding area.

As community colleges became more widespread, their missions began to diverge in response to the specific needs of their communities. At the same time, higher education as a whole was beginning to reawaken to the notion of giving back to the community, both by establishing community service/partnership programs and by educating students to be active citizens. Although some critics have taken community colleges to task for focusing too closely on workforce readiness and other goals at the expense of community engagement, community colleges by their nature remain tied to their communities on many levels.

Table 1:
U.S. Community College Growth by Decade, 1901 – 2000

DECADE	NEW COLLEGES	TOTAL NUMBER OF COMMUNITY COLLEGES
1901 – 1910	25	25
1911 – 1920	49	74
1921 – 1930	106	180
1931 – 1940	58	238
1941 – 1950	92	330
1951 – 1960	82	412
1961 – 1970	497	909
1971 – 1980	149	1,058
1981 – 1990	48	1,106
1991 – 2000	49	1,155

Source: Phillippe, K.A., & Patton, M. (2000). *National Profile of Community Colleges: Trends and Statistics.* Washington, DC: Community College Press.

A Tradition of Innovation

Although America's community colleges recently celebrated their 100th anniversary, they are still considered the new kids on the block of higher education. This perception of newness is shaped by three factors. First, nearly two thirds of all community colleges trace their origins either to the social upheaval of the 1960s (43%) or to the three decades that followed (21%) (see Table 1).

Second, community colleges are the fastest growing sector of American higher education. The proportion of

U.S. undergraduate students attending a public two-year college increased from 28.7% in 1972 to 37.0% in 1992 (Calhoun, 1999) to 44.0% in 2000 (Phillippe and Patton, 2000). These figures reflect growth compared with total enrollment in four-year institutions; if just the first two years of enrollment at four-year institutions were the point of comparison, the proportional growth of community college enrollments would be even more dramatic.

Third, the types of students who enroll in community colleges are often "new"; that is, first-generation college students, older students, or students from low-income communities who have traditionally found tuition at baccalaureate institutions out of reach. According to the American Association of Community Colleges' most recent fact sheet (available at www.aacc.nche.edu), the 5.4 million for-credit students enrolled in America's community colleges represent a broadly diverse population, including 46% of black, 55% of Hispanic, 46% of Asian/Pacific Islander, and 55% of Native American undergraduate students. This diversity extends to age as well. The average age of community college students is 29; only 40% are under age 22, and more than 15% are over age 40 (Phillippe and Patton, 2000).

Although the upstart image of community colleges sometimes leads to a certain kind of condescension on the part of older educational institutions, the qualities that distinguish community colleges as "new" confer a number of advantages. In many ways, community colleges comprise the most nimble and responsive sector of American higher education. This responsiveness is evident in the multiple missions they have undertaken. A sample list of missions would include providing a gathering place where diversity is celebrated; facilitating transfer to a baccalaureate program; offering occupational education, developmental education, adult basic education, English as a second language, international education, customized training for specific companies, non-credit instruction, and small business development; preparing students for industry certification exams as well as lifelong learning; offering education and training for welfare recipients and others facing serious barriers to employment; and preparing students for lives of civic engagement (Bailey and Weininger, 2002).

In many ways, community colleges comprise the most nimble and responsive sector of American higher education.

Fulfilling such a broad range of missions is a difficult task, but being able to expand, adapt, or add to their mission in response to local needs is a core practice of civically engaged community colleges. Community colleges sponsor town hall meetings to address issues of local concern, offer free or low-cost English language instruction in communities with large populations for whom English is a second language, create community health initiatives, and provide day care centers in areas where low-cost childcare can mean the difference between economic development and welfare. They include community members on their advisory boards and steering committees. They form partnerships with local agencies that work to assist distressed neighborhoods. In these ways and more they adapt their missions and their work to the needs of their communities.

Another advantage of "newness"—one that will become more important as the nation's demographics continue to change—is the ability of community colleges to accommodate students from widely diverse backgrounds. Bailey and Weininger (2002, p. 3) note that community colleges are designed to "facilitate access to higher education for all groups, including individuals with weak academic skills, low incomes, and other characteristics that create barriers to further education." As American society becomes increasingly diverse in the decades ahead, and as four-year colleges and universities remain prohibitively expensive for most low-income students, community colleges will increasingly become the access point to higher education for lower and perhaps middle income students (Franco, 2002a).

With community colleges increasingly taking on the mission of providing access to higher education for all Americans, their role as civic leaders in their communities has become even more vital. The community colleges featured in this monograph are among those that go beyond meeting the immediate needs of their students and their communities to providing leadership for positive social and economic change (Musil, 2003). These colleges recognize that the social, intellectual, and financial capital they bring to local partnerships can transform communities and increase opportunity for everyone.

The State of Engagement at Community Colleges

The majority of America's more than 1,100 community colleges engage in service through volunteer programs, student clubs, and organizations such as Phi Theta Kappa (the community college National Honor Society). Most community colleges are also committed to experiential pedagogies, such as cooperative education, clinicals, practica, and internships—many of which are related to their workforce preparation missions. Through the work of the League for Innovation in the Community College, the American Association of Community Colleges (AACC)—especially through its Community Colleges Broadening Horizons through Service-Learning project—and the Community College National Center for Community Engagement (CCNCCE; formerly the Campus Compact National Center for Community Colleges), many two-year colleges have introduced active learning classroom pedagogies as well as Internet and web-based experiential learning.

Service-learning—the practice of making community engagement part of a course curriculum—is somewhat less well developed at community colleges, but it is gaining in importance. By the mid-1990s, hundreds of community colleges had begun to re-emphasize their civic role through the adoption of service-learning as a pedagogy. Surveys conducted by the AACC between 1995 and 2001 indicate that nearly half of all community colleges offer service-learning and that 40% of faculty surveyed are interested in this teaching and learning method (Gottlieb and Robinson, 2002). AACC's most recent member survey found that the number of community colleges using service-learning more than doubled between 1995 and 2003 (Prentice,

WEB RESOURCES FOR ENGAGEMENT AT COMMUNITY COLLEGES

The American Association of Community Colleges
www.aacc.nche.edu. This website features important statistics about community colleges, a national community college database, current news and legislative issues, and pertinent web and print resources.

The American Association for Higher Education
www.aahe.org. AAHE's website offers online access to *Change* magazine as well as news and information about the association's other publications and events.

The Association of American Colleges and Universities
www.aacu-edu.org. This website provides resources, initiatives, publications, and conferences pertaining to key issues in higher education, including civic engagement.

Campus Compact
www.compact.org. In addition to providing valuable resources about legislation, campus-community partnerships, and grants and fellowships for community engagement, this site features databases of model programs at community colleges and information about the Indicators of Engagement Project. (See also www.compact.org/community-colleges.)

The Community College National Center for Community Engagement
www.mc.maricopa.edu/other/engagement. This website gives information about CCNCCE's conferences and publications and provides online access to the *Journal for Civic Commitment* as well as descriptions of model service-learning projects at community colleges throughout the country.

The Education Commission of the States
www.ecs.org. This site includes facts, current debates, web resources, and ECS projects relating to a large number of issues facing postsecondary education.

The League for Innovation in the Community College
www.league.org/welcome.htm. This website provides information about the League, its membership, conferences, publications, and initiatives, as well as community college resources on the Internet.

The National Education Association Higher Education Program
www.nea.org/he/heprog.html. This website provides information about membership and current topics in higher education as well as access to leadership tools and online journals.

National Institute for Staff and Organizational Development
www.nisod.org. NISOD focuses on professional development opportunities for community college faculty, staff, and administrators, with an emphasis on improving teaching and learning. The website provides information on NISOD conferences and publications as well as other resources related to teaching and learning.

Robinson, and McPhee, 2003). A recent AACC Project Brief found that chief academic officers (CAOs) at community colleges strongly associate service-learning with enhanced student learning and that "in the face of the most severe budget cuts many had ever experienced, all affirmed that service-learning will be sustained on their campuses" (Prentice, Exley, and Robinson, 2003, p. 6).

Most community colleges that offer service-learning do so in the form of service-learning components integrated within existing courses. Far fewer offer courses where service-learning is required of all students and where civic responsibility is a specified learning outcome. Furthermore, service-learning in community colleges is usually a response to specific community issues such as diversity, early literacy, health, teacher preparation, homelessness, and hunger. A small percentage of community colleges explicitly state that they use service-learning to achieve the broader goal of educating students for the work of democracy.

Because community colleges usually do not have in-house fund developers to seek grant support for their service-learning programs, sustainability and growth have been difficult to achieve. Coordinating efforts across campus into an integrated strategy presents additional challenges. Organizations such as AACC, Campus Compact, and CCNCCE are working to help community colleges develop coordinated service-learning and civic engagement strategies and are providing important professional development opportunities for faculty and administrators. All of these organizations have useful websites, publications, and other resources. Regional and national workshops, institutes, and conferences provide cyclical planning and professional development opportunities for campuses. Campus Compact also has 30 state offices that provide local training and support.

The importance of civic engagement is becoming ever more widely recognized across higher education.

The Movement Toward Greater Engagement

The importance of civic engagement—beyond scattershot service efforts—is becoming ever more widely recognized across higher education. New regional accreditation standards, such as those at the Accrediting Commission for Community and Junior Colleges in the western region and the Council of North Central Two-Year Colleges, now include explicit language requiring attention to preparing students for ethical, responsible citizenship. Higher education associations, including Campus Compact, the Association of American Colleges and Universities (AAC&U), the American Association for Higher Education (AAHE), the National Education Association (NEA), and the Education Commission of the States (ECS), are recognizing the growing influence of community colleges while renewing their own emphasis on civic engagement in a diverse democracy.

Campus Compact has devoted substantial time and resources to promoting education for democracy. The rationale for this work is articulated in the *Presidents' Declaration on the Civic Responsibility of Higher Education* (Campus Compact, 1999, 2004), written by a group of college and university presidents and signed by hundreds of presidents from across the country. The Declaration states, in part, that:

> This country cannot afford to educate a generation that acquires knowledge without ever understanding how that knowledge can benefit society or influence democratic decision-making. We must teach the skills and values of democracy, creating innumerable opportunities for our students to practice and reap the results of the real, hard work of citizenship.

Compact resources and initiatives in this endeavor include national and state-level advocacy and legislative work; grants to disciplinary associations to further their commitment to service-learning; direct training for community service/service-learning directors and faculty; resources such as program models, syllabi, and publications (e.g., the *Introduction to Service-Learning Toolkit, second edition,* and the

Engaged Department Toolkit); the student-focused Raise Your Voice campaign to boost civic participation; and national awards programs that recognize and honor engaged faculty and students.

In addition to these resources and programs, Campus Compact has partnered with AAHE to deepen service-learning and civic engagement in academic departments through the monograph series *Service-Learning in the Disciplines.* Now at 19 volumes, this series continues to expand. Most monographs contain chapters authored by community college faculty that focus on the particular challenges and opportunities they face in incorporating service-learning into their academic discipline in a community college context.

Other organizations have also published important works on this topic. AAC&U's Greater Expectations initiative, for example, emphasizes practical liberal learning that prepares students for active democratic participation. In May 2003, the entire edition of AAC&U's journal *Peer Review* was devoted to the topic of educating students for democracy, and the association recently published a monograph entitled *Civic Engagement in a Diverse Democracy.* In addition, the summer 2003 edition of the NEA's higher education journal *Thought and Action* features an essay by Woodruff D. Smith entitled "Higher Education, Democracy, and the Public Sphere." Clearly, this issue is on the minds of many of today's academic leaders.

A Future of Challenge and Possibility

America's cultural geography is changing rapidly and radically. No longer do Americans enjoy the freedom of job security and stable communities. As Americans change jobs and communities over the course of their lives, it becomes more and more difficult to sense and experience civic engagement. Given this growing social disconnection and mobility, it is more important than ever before that community colleges continue to be places where Americans find community and opportunity.

America's cultural geography is now global. Community colleges, America's truly unique higher education institutions, have a bright future on the international landscape, as developed and developing democracies try to reach a larger proportion of their populations with both transfer and vocational education. In Thailand, for example, 10 new community colleges have been established in the last two years, with assistance from the University of Hawaii community college system. In January 2004, the International Partnerships in Service Learning organization is sponsoring a major conference in Thailand. Community colleges, America's democracy colleges, should be well-represented.

Because of their many close ties to their communities, community colleges are uniquely positioned to become civic engagement leaders at home and abroad, both in principle and in practice. As the examples in this monograph demonstrate, many community colleges have taken on this challenge. These colleges, which often do this work with little outside acknowledgment or support, have important lessons to share with all of American higher education.

Institutional Culture

Although all community colleges are nominally of their communities, a wide spectrum of possibilities exists for understanding and acting on this connection. In this chapter we examine those indicators that help establish a felt culture of engagement, a culture that demonstrably affects the way in which faculty, students, and community partners experience the goals and priorities of the college. We begin with statements—formal and informal—that define the purpose, vision, and work of colleges whose culture intentionally fosters engagement, and then proceed to look at some of the ways in which administrative leaders act upon those statements. The indicators discussed in this section include *mission and purpose* and *administrative and academic leadership.*

Mission and Purpose

Best Practices

- Include civic/community engagement in the college's mission statement.
- Write and/or speak publicly about the community role of higher education and of the college itself.
- Create opportunities for faculty and staff to participate in community events.
- Make community partners welcome as part of the campus community; invite them to join advisory boards and other participatory forums.

THE INDICATORS DEFINED: MISSION AND PURPOSE

- The college's mission explicitly articulates its commitment to the public purposes of higher education and higher education's civic responsibility to educate for democratic participation.
- This aspect of the mission is openly valued and is explicitly used to promote and to explain the civic activities of the campus.
- The college demonstrates a genuine willingness to review, discuss, and strengthen the civic aspect of its mission.
- All campus constituencies demonstrate their familiarity with and ownership of the college's mission.

The Indicators in Action

Among the colleges we looked at, we found several where the institution's mission statement makes explicit its commitment to civic engagement. Mission statements like those from Portland Community College and Malcolm X College (see sidebar) articulate a responsibility to prepare students not only for individual success but also for participation in a democratic society and global citizenship. Such goals are not left to be inferred through references to general education and personal growth. Instead, they are singled out for public emphasis.

This same kind of emphasis characterizes many of the public statements of Eduardo Padrón, President of Miami Dade College (formerly Miami-Dade Community College). In a recent essay, Padrón begins with the statement, "If you were to ask what Miami Dade College does, I would reply that our fundamental purpose is to preserve democracy." He then goes on to spell out the many ways in which Miami Dade tries to do this with and for its approximately 130,000 students. Although service-learning is only one among many strategies the college employs, "It [provides] the most striking example of Miami Dade College's commitment to make a difference in the lives of our students and community **by focusing on the development of civic literacy"** [emphasis added].

**EXAMPLES FROM THE FIELD:
MISSION STATEMENTS WITH CIVIC EMPHASIS**

"Through effective teaching and supportive student services, Portland Community College prepares students for success as individuals, members of a democratic society, and citizens of a rapidly changing world."

—From the Portland Community College mission statement

"Our mission is to empower each individual to be all he or she is capable of becoming through quality, comprehensive, and affordable educational programs and services. An important goal of the mission is to enhance the quality of life of an economically, educationally, culturally, and socially diverse community."

—From the Malcolm X College 2002 Annual Report, p. 3

This same theme sounds in the words of another president, one whose college is in many ways the antithesis of Miami Dade. Kirtland Community College, a small, rural school in Roscommon, Michigan, demonstrates that one need not be located at the forefront of American demographic change to recognize the civic imperative in the work of community colleges. As Kirtland's president, Charles Rorie, remarks of his school's progress toward engagement:

> We know an engaged campus is committed to initiating, increasing, and enhancing community service opportunities locally, regionally, and nationally. To create an engaged citizenry our students must be nurtured by an engaged campus.... We have experienced successes and failures, yet the commitment to service will outlast the tenure of a president or a generation of faculty. It will endure the possibility of future budget cuts. It must, because democracy cannot long survive without the participation of its citizens.

To be effective, the mission of such an "engaged campus" must find strong public resonance. At Malcolm X College in Chicago, the school's mission—"Empowerment through Education"—derives directly from the words of its namesake and his vision of community empowerment. Thus, the school's community partners pay it a supreme compliment when they note, as one community partner did, that they themselves "feel like [a] part of Malcolm X." Even the community's disenfranchised are seen as potential members of the college community. As another community partner noted, "We have 18,000 homeless people we serve and we want them to eventually transfer to Malcolm X...to empower themselves." At Malcolm X, the phrase "Empowerment through Education" appears on all sorts of printed materials—even on faculty syllabi.

To be effective, the mission of an "engaged campus" must find strong public resonance.

When, at community colleges like these, the civic dimension of the institution's mission statement plays such a visible, shaping role, it is only to be expected that it will inform a variety of key institutional documents. At Middlesex Community College in Massachusetts, the mission statement's explicit emphasis on community partnerships helped pave the way for a "professional day" during which faculty met with the administration to discuss the link between service-learning and the school's strategic planning process. One sub-committee session bore the title "Fostering Civic Engagement and Community Partnerships on a Local and Global Level."

At Chandler-Gilbert Community College in Arizona, President Maria Hesse's *Strategic Plan 2002–2007* identifies community engagement as one of the college's key strategic directions: "CGCC will strive to promote community service and civic engagement." The document also identifies "college interaction with community" and "opportunities for students, faculty, and staff to engage in community service and other civic activities" as institutional priorities. Objectives related to these priorities include "Increase participation of college personnel in community events" and "Develop opportunities for community participation in college activities and advisory boards."

Like many of the other schools described here, Portland Community College's commitment to community engagement has long been a part of the school's mission. However, its 2001 mission revision took this commitment a step farther by including a new emphasis on outcomes-based approaches. As part of this effort, Portland established five core areas of student learning: critical thinking and problem solving, communication, community and environmental responsibility, self-reflection, and cultural awareness. Although the new core areas help to define the college's connection to the community more explicitly, community stakeholders have never questioned Portland's commitment to the community. One community member noted that President Carreon is "very visible at the state higher education level" while another partner mentioned that the president spoke at various fairs and receptions for service and service-learning.

In another example, President Carey Israel began his administration at Collin County Community College District in Texas with a district-wide process of redefining the institution's fundamental values. Collin County now lists "service and involvement" prominently among its core values, calling such engagement an institutional "passion."

What all of these examples highlight is that colleges with a mission and purpose that support civic engagement are able to create a culture in which community concerns and civic literacy figure as considerations of primary value—that is, considerations that are important in themselves and not merely the assumed result of other, more traditional educational goals. However, for such a culture to come alive, it must also be embodied in the concrete actions of the administrative and academic leadership.

Administrative and Academic Leadership

Best Practices

- Ensure that administrative and academic leaders are directly involved in both internal and external service initiatives.
- Assign responsibility for community relations to a specific staff member with administrative responsibility.
- Create policies and procedures for faculty hiring, retention, and recognition that reward community work.
- Build support for engagement among board members.

THE INDICATORS DEFINED: ACADEMIC AND ADMINISTRATIVE LEADERSHIP

- The president, the chief academic officer, and the trustees visibly support campus civic engagement, in both their words and their actions.
- The president and the college's academic leaders have played a visible and committed role in helping the college evolve into a genuinely engaged institution.
- The campus is publicly regarded as an important and reliable partner in local community development efforts.

The Indicators in Action

Again and again in our conversations with a wide range of community college stakeholders, we heard how presidents, chief academic officers, and deans not only "talked the talk" but "walked the walk." Asked about his own degree of involvement with the local community, Miami Dade President Padrón lamented, "My involvement is overwhelming.... It's difficult for me to say 'No.'" Asked the same question, Middlesex Community College President Carole Cowan quipped, "Follow me around some day." Cowan currently sits on 20–30 community boards and was described by one of her deans "as a kind of ombudsperson—supporting community ideas through resource allocations."

Portland Community College has an administrative position expressly designed to help realize and develop the college's stated commitment to community engagement.

As Community Relations Manager Neal Naigus put it, his role is to act as "the eyes and ears of the president in the community." But his activities extend well beyond looking and listening. He is also responsible for brokering the college's services to the community, identifying and developing community partnerships, organizing public forums, and acting as a community resource. As Naigus points out, "[the] position is an indication of the college's civic commitment."

Such statements of commitment are typical for many of the presidents and senior administrators we interviewed, but what makes them especially significant is the fact that, out of the president's or the dean's earshot, faculty members and community partners repeatedly confirmed their accuracy. Indeed, many community partners noted that specific college personnel created community opportunities that would not have been available without their support. One unique example is Chandler-Gilbert's involvement in the creation of the Boys and Girls Club housed on the college's Williams Campus. Many students volunteer at the club as part of their community service and service-learning projects.

However, external initiatives are not the only items that find a place on these administrators' calendars. At Chandler-Gilbert, President Hesse and her staff also make a point of showing up for the college's "Days of Service" and of sitting in on the reflection sessions of service-learning classes. Similarly, at Albuquerque Technical Vocational Institute (TVI), administrators regularly join as many as 200 students, faculty, and community partners for yearly service-learning reflection sessions. Through the input and feedback they get directly from the community, Albuquerque TVI's administrative leaders are able to increase the responsiveness of the college's service activities while at the same time demonstrating their own leadership and commitment.

Personal participation is one way in which administrative and academic leaders can signal their support for civic engagement. The policies they help formulate, promote, and implement are another. Especially important in this regard are policies and procedures concerning faculty hiring, retention, and recognition. Again and again we found at colleges committed to civic engagement a deliberate strategy for identifying and retaining faculty who shared this commitment. At Kapi'olani Community College in Hawaii, Provost John Morton describes how, over several years, the college has consciously recruited and cultivated faculty "who actively engage in community-related work." Through a skillful use of hiring practices, new faculty orientations, promotional materials and workshops, faculty evaluation forms, and contract renewal guidelines, Kapi'olani has succeeded in establishing community-related work as a "defining value of the college."

Again and again we found at colleges committed to civic engagement a deliberate strategy for identifying and retaining faculty who shared this commitment.

At Raritan Valley Community College, President Jerry Ryan spoke of working to "build a new breed of faculty member," with whom public commitment personally resonates—while at the same time acknowledging the ways in which his senior faculty have responded enthusiastically to this emphasis. By creating a professional culture in which community-related work is accepted as institutionally valued and academically valid, effective administrative and academic leaders short-circuit much of the faculty resistance against which other schools constantly struggle.

Campus Compact's annual member surveys clearly document the impact of faculty attitudes toward civic engagement on the success of campus programs. In the 2000 survey, almost one half of all respondents (48%) cited faculty resistance to curricular changes as an obstacle to the institutionalization or advancement of service-learning. Over the past few years, this percentage has dropped slowly but steadily, reaching 36% in 2002. While this decline is encouraging, faculty resistance to service-learning clearly remains one of the most significant obstacles to the institutionalization of service-learning on campus.

Thus, the fact that at Malcolm X College the administration maintains an exceptionally congenial and cooperative relationship with the various unions representing the college's faculty and staff is worth special notice. Clearly exemplifying this relationship is the *2000–2004 Four Year Agreement* established by the college's board and its faculty union. Strong, clear, respectful communication between administrators and faculty groups creates the kind of environment that is conducive to effective, concerted action.

But if faculty and community partner perceptions of an institution and its commitment to civic engagement matter, so too does its students' understanding of the college's commitment. Several students interviewed at Malcolm X noted the ubiquitousness of the college's mission. One put it this way: "You can feel its presence." Students at Kapi'olani Community College reported that their college's commitment to the community was similarly palpable. And because community-based work is such a defining feature of Kapi'olani's identity, students noted that they arrived on campus fully expecting to be involved themselves. Students interviewed at Raritan Valley also confirmed their college's support for engagement, identifying a "groundswell movement" toward service-learning on their campus. They also commented on the wide range of civic engagement projects available to them and expressed enthusiasm about their community-based experiences.

Facilitating the growth of civic engagement by creating appropriate channels for its expression can be a very important part of administrative leadership.

Facilitating the growth of civic engagement by creating appropriate channels for its expression can be a very important part of administrative leadership. Since one explicit objective in Chandler-Gilbert's strategic plan is to "increase participation of college personnel in community events," President Hesse's office must ensure that such opportunities exist. The college's "days of service" program, in which *all* college stakeholders—administration, faculty, staff, and students—are encouraged to participate, represents one such opportunity. Brevard Community College makes available to its faculty and staff a service opportunity not available at many other schools.

Brevard grants faculty and staff a paid weekly "wellness break," and employees have the option of devoting their wellness time to on- or off-campus service activities.

Closely related to such leadership through facilitation is leadership through resource management. At Miami Dade College, President Padrón identifies his ability and willingness to sustain his college's service-learning program as a point of particular pride. As he pointed out, since his school has lost 300 positions since 1996, "It would have been easy to eliminate service-learning... If there's one thing I've done that's difficult, it's to make service-learning integral to the curriculum."

Other presidents have made similar bottom-line decisions in difficult economic times and have refused to sacrifice civic engagement to economic expediency. That they have been able to do so generally reflects the skillful ways in which they have built support among their boards of directors. For example, at Raritan Valley, two successive presidents have worked so effectively with the board that the board members are now at least as supportive of civic engagement as is the administration, and many board members are themselves civically engaged. At Kirtland, President Rorie makes information about the college's civic engagement efforts a regular part of his board briefings. As a result, the board has become an enthusiastic supporter of those efforts.

When talking to presidents and other top administrators, one sometimes hears the disclaimer that the individual in question prefers not to "impose" his/her will on the faculty and other college constituencies. But the alternative to "imposing one's will" is not inaction. Most of the administrators we spoke with are both respected and admired by their constituencies. Their leadership is not seen as arbitrary but as visionary. Indeed, what was perhaps most surprising was the degree to which a powerful commitment to the larger community so often went hand in hand with a fine sensitivity to the campus community.

Curriculum & Pedagogy

ne of the most important lessons of the last decade has been that civic engagement must be rooted in the core work of a college or university if it is to be spread effectively across the institution. Since the core work of most colleges is teaching and learning, civic engagement must be linked directly to their curricula if it is to achieve full acceptance. At a community college, this link is especially important. Not only do many commuter students need the legitimacy of a curricular tie to get them involved in activities outside the classroom, they also need to see civic engagement linked to the development of those workplace skills they came to the college to acquire.

Many commuter students need to see civic engagement linked to the development of those workplace skills they came to the college to acquire.

Hence, for many community colleges committed to civic engagement, that commitment requires a well developed service-learning program. Raritan Valley Community College's strategic plan for 2003–2008 identifies as a "Tier 1" initiative:

> Catalyze civic engagement and community service opportunities by identifying and supporting students, faculty, staff, administrators, and community members who develop creative and effective approaches to active citizenship.

Putting this initiative into action will involve at least three complementary strategies: (1) crossing boundaries between credit and non-credit programs and between academic and cultural instruction; (2) integrating the efforts of special programs and centers at the college such as The Institute of Holocaust and Genocide Studies and The Paul Robeson Institute of Ethics, Leadership, and Social Justice; and (3) service-learning.

Similarly, because Brevard Community College believes that "community service is an important way to prepare students for their roles as responsible citizens," it has developed "an infrastructure to support a comprehensive service-learning program" (Henry, 1998, p. 84). Portland Community College lists "community and environmental responsibility" as one of the core outcomes the college seeks to foster in its students, and views service-learning as an important method of realizing that goal.

At Anne Arundel Community College, the college emphasizes the importance of a "students first," learning-centered approach to education, and actualizes this philosophy in part through its service-learning program. Like Portland, Anne Arundel lists "social and civic responsibility" as one of the core competencies for its students.

And yet, as useful as service-learning can be as a vehicle of civic engagement, it is not automatically effective. Just as civic engagement is possible without a curricular vehicle (e.g., Raritan Valley's other two strategies, identified above), so service-learning can entail community engagement without any strong emphasis on *civic* awareness. While it seems likely that any well designed service-learning program will necessarily raise students' awareness of community resources and needs (since any such activity will require them to reflect on their experiences), not all courses or programs explicitly tie that awareness to the competencies and responsibilities needed to sustain a democracy. Middlesex Community College President Carole Cowan can boast one of the most well established service-learning programs in the country, yet she acknowledges that civic engagement is a relatively new emphasis, an area in which "the college is evolving."

In the pages that follow, we identify many curricular initiatives that clearly lay a foundation for civic engagement. However, we do not thereby mean to imply that in every instance the activities identified necessarily include a fully developed *civic,* as distinct from *community,* component. Indeed, as we shall see, the ways in which the colleges we looked at conceptualize and implement service-learning raise many interesting questions about possible intersections between civic and community concerns.

Disciplines, Departments, and Interdisciplinary Work

Best Practices

- Enlist department chairs to encourage adoption of engaged practices throughout the department and discipline.
- Work with a community partner to organize projects around a complex community initiative.
- Partner with workforce development and other learning-based programs.
- Create forums for interdisciplinary communication and cooperation.
- Give individual faculty time to devote to service and leeway in developing service-learning initiatives.

The Indicators in Action

One of the easiest ways to gauge the vitality of a service-learning program is to look at not only the number of service-learning courses it offers, but also the extent to which those courses are representative of the curriculum as a whole. In the case of Raritan Valley and Brevard, both the number and the representativeness of the courses are impressive. Brevard, for example, boasted well over 100 courses and over 250 course sections in more than 40 disciplines by the late 1990s. In 2002–2003 those numbers had grown to more than 135 courses and 350 course sections. According to Raritan Valley's service-learning brochure, the college is one of only two institutions in the country "where the majority of the faculty members are actively involved in the institution's service-learning program." The same publication identifies 24 disciplinary areas that participate in that program. The figures for several of the other schools we looked at are similarly impressive. For instance, Portland Community College offers service-learning courses in 43 disciplines. Kapi'olani lists 69 service-learning courses for the Spring 2003 semester, and Miami Dade offers 90 service-learning courses each academic year.

THE INDICATORS DEFINED: DISCIPLINES, DEPARTMENTS, AND INTERDISCIPLINARY WORK

- Community-based learning opportunities can be found across the entire curriculum. It is as much the concern of the arts and humanities, the natural sciences, technical disciplines, pre-professional studies, and interdisciplinary programs as it is of the social sciences.
- Students have multiple opportunities to do community-based work in their general education and career (vocational, technical, occupational) curricula.
- Formal opportunities exist for capstone experiences (group reflection meetings, forums, variable credit courses, capstones often not credited by the university other than as elective credit) focused on community-based problems or issues in most disciplines.
- Academic units (i.e., departments and programs) rather than individual faculty members have assumed ownership of partnering activities.
- Course-based community initiatives are structured and/or coordinated across disciplines, such as learning communities, cohort and peer approaches, and thematically linked courses across semesters.

Another indication of service-learning's vitality on a given campus is the degree to which it has been embraced by multiple members of the same department and/or discipline, especially when this group interest translates into a coherent larger design. One of the best examples we found of this strength was the nursing program at Raritan Valley, which requires its students to participate in service-learning experiences in each of their first three semesters. As a part of their required service-learning components, nursing students have assisted with immunizations at local clinics, provided home health care to the elderly, and researched and documented the 50-year history of the Somerset Valley Visiting Nurses Association. These experiences are designed to be cumulative and to expose students "to a side of nursing different from the acute care they experience in clinical settings," as one professor put it.

"The key seems to be the naturalness of fit between the curriculum and the service."

Some disciplines tend to be especially conducive to service-learning and to benefit very clearly from such a curricular component. Nursing, of course, is such a discipline, and in addition to Raritan Valley's program we came across several other nursing programs that demonstrated widespread departmental commitment. At Miami Dade College, the English as a second language (ESL) program is similarly involved because, as one faculty member observed, service-learning "works so well there." At Portland Community College the same is true of the sociology department; as community relations manager Neal Naigus noted, this is in part because the discipline

EXAMPLE FROM THE FIELD: COURSES WITH A SERVICE COMPONENT

Following is a sampling of courses at Brevard Community College that include a service component.

- Accounting
- Advertising
- Algebra
- American History
- Anatomy & Physiology
- Art History, Design
- Biology
- Business Communications
- Calculus
- Chemistry
- Communications I & II
- Computer Repair
- Criminology
- Economics II
- Education
- Environmental Science
- Finance
- Fundamentals of Speech
- Graphic Design
- History I & II
- Hospitality Management
- International Study
- Leadership
- Marketing
- Micro Computer Apps
- Microbiology
- Music
- Nursing
- Oceanography
- Philosophy
- Political Science
- Psychology
- Social Science I & II
- Social Work
- Sociology I
- Spanish III & IV
- Statistics
- Theatre
- Trigonometry
- Veterinary Technology
- World Religions

—From Brevard Community College

lends itself to social activism. "The key seems to be the naturalness of fit between the curriculum and the service," he observed.

At some colleges, service-learning has been incorporated into science programs with impressive results. For example, Southern Maine Community College's department of applied marine biology and oceanography has integrated service-learning into every course offered. The service-learning program is organized around a set of ongoing community projects, and classes enter into these projects in a variety of ways. Ongoing community projects include the Alewife Restoration Project, which is exploring why the alewives stopped spawning in Great Pond in Cape Elizabeth, Maine, and is working to reintroduce the species; the Brown Trout Program, in which aquaculture students grow brown trout while students in introductory biology classes tag and release the fish; and the Lobster Program, where the college has taken charge of one of the Lobster Conservancy's sites for observing lobster population shifts while marine science students grow baby lobsters and donate them to the Conservancy. According to Jack Nye, a professor of marine science, the department deliberately chose service-learning as an umbrella for its marine science courses both to create continuity between courses and to allow students to experience multiple service projects and sites within their departmental coursework. The department's website (www.smtc.net/programs/marinescience.htm) discusses this service-learning component and emphasizes the active role students play in the marine science major.

To promote greater depth of faculty commitment, colleges need to be more deliberate in targeting discipline-based units and departments.

While organized and concerted efforts across a department are generally to be desired, a strong departmental commitment to service-learning is more often driven by the dedication and hard work of individual faculty members. Such is the case at Middlesex Community College where, for example, the college's extensive service-learning program places a primary emphasis on individual faculty initiative. The college supports this emphasis, allowing faculty members time they can devote to service and giving them considerable leeway in defining their service-learning activities. Faculty have responded to this freedom with enthusiasm and creativity.

Still, for the most part, we found departmental/disciplinary concentrations relatively rare. It is not unusual for a faculty member in a given discipline or department to be the only individual using service-learning in his or her unit. Hence, in order to promote greater depth of faculty commitment and to make possible more cumulative, developmental student experiences, colleges need to be more deliberate in targeting discipline-based units and departments. Anne Arundel Community College's dean for learning advancement, Trish Casey-Whiteman, has acknowledged this need, but has also pointed out that her college is working toward replicating nursing's successful approach in other departments: "Faculty members are working to push programs up to the departmental level." According to Portland Community College's community relations manager Neal Naigus, the college's computer science and psychology departments aim to have all of their courses involved in service-learning within the next three years.

Such targeted development is precisely what Miami Dade had in mind when it became the first community college to host a Campus Compact Engaged Department Institute in March 2003. Participating in the three-day event were 20 departmental teams from five of the college's six campuses. Most teams included the department chair, several faculty members, and a community partner chosen by the department for the relevance of its work to departmental responsibilities and interests. By the end of the three days, each team had not only deepened its understanding of service-learning as a teaching/learning

EXAMPLE FROM THE FIELD: ENGAGED DEPARTMENT INSTITUTE ANNOUNCEMENT

Why Attend

- Earn 18 professional development hours
- Explore how service-learning can work in your department
- Create a department-wide community partnership
- Deepen your understanding of service-learning, civic engagement, and campus-community partnerships
- Expand your teaching/learning repertoire
- Discover how to benefit your students and the community simultaneously
- Learn how to prepare students for success—personally, professionally, and as citizens

Description of Institute

The purpose of the Institute is to help participating departments develop strategies to:

1. Include community-based work in their teaching/learning strategies
2. Explore the possibility of including community-based experiences as an expectation for majors
3. Identify a community need and community agency related to departmental teaching/learning goals
4. Create a department-level partnership with the identified agency to address the need
5. Develop a level of coherence within the department to model civic engagement and progressive change

Workshop Topics

- Develop strategies to include community-based work in both teaching and scholarship
- Develop a model of civic engagement and progressive change at the departmental level
- Describe various discipline-specific models of service-learning integration
- Determine an array of assessment techniques for community-based work on both the faculty and student level
- Support community-based work on both the faculty and student level
- Explain how community-based work is a vehicle of curricular integration
- Describe how community partners and departments are resources for one another
- Create a departmental action plan to implement a community-faculty partnership

—From Miami Dade College

strategy, it had also developed "a model of civic engagement and progressive change at the departmental level"—complete with a timeline and assessment strategy. The event also helped a wide range of departments compare notes on their work and may have set the stage for possible interdisciplinary work in the future.

Like departmental programs, projects organized around complex community initiatives can also create links between courses, foster a more lasting relationship between the college and the community, and increase the significance of the service activity for both the agency and the student. At the College of Lake County in Illinois, for example, a special channel of communication has been opened between the college and the local United Way. The United Way chapter has a very active volunteer center, and thanks to a personal relationship with the director of placement and career services, Terri Berryman, the center is able to convey its needs to the college in a way that helps focus student community engagement.

Chandler-Gilbert Community College's partnership with its local Boys and Girls Club is another good example of focused attention. As Mike Greene, former Boys and Girls Club director (and current director of student life at Chandler-Gilbert), noted, the club, which is actually housed on Chandler-Gilbert's Williams Campus, has "been with the [service-learning] program from the beginning"—a rather impressive fact given the long-established nature of the college's service-learning effort.

At Southern Maine Community College, the nonprofit organization Friends of Casco Bay also has space directly on the campus. Such an arrangement allows students of the college's marine science department to take part in the agency's stewardship activities and to assist in monitoring water quality in adjacent Casco Bay. Thus, marine science models both departmental and project-based organizational strategies.

At the other end of the "convenience" spectrum, Johnson County Community College in Kansas has established an important long-term relationship with the Mexican community of Las Pintas. Having learned about the community at an international conference, the college evaluated its suitability as a service-learning site, and in 1988 sent a team of 12 students and 6 faculty for a week-long stay. During that first visit, most members of the college group built walls, while a nursing instructor began making home visits. On subsequent visits, however, the college team included both nursing and dental hygiene students—directly as a result of what the school had learned about local needs. Now the college sends two groups to Las Pintas every year, including participants from its early childhood program; its heating, ventilation, and air conditioning program; and Spanish language students who serve as translators.

Still a third strategy for engagement beyond the individual course involves developing synergy with other learning-based programs. While pre-employment, field-specific, and other workforce development programs seek to achieve outcomes other than civic engagement, the way in which they benefit multiple stakeholders nonetheless parallels service-learning. By placing students in a situation where they can quickly and effectively acquire valuable real-world experience, and by placing student skills at the disposal of local businesses, workforce development efforts can also strengthen communities. As Middlesex Community College President Carole Cowan puts it, "Workforce development is a legitimate form of engagement." Both workforce development and service-learning programs can maximize their effectiveness by recognizing those features they have in common and acting cooperatively.

EXAMPLE FROM THE FIELD: INTERDISCIPLINARY WORK

"RVCC builds community by crossing the boundaries between credit and non-credit programs and between academic and cultural instruction. As a community-based institution, RVCC offers degree and certificate programs that fulfill the community's need for public servants. A sampling of such academic programs includes: nursing, criminal justice, paralegal studies, and early childhood education. The Corporate and Continuing Education division of the College provides comprehensive, quality, and innovative education programs, including training and other professional services that encourage and support workforce development and life-long learning. This has a positive impact on the economic development of our region."

—From Raritan Valley Community College, "It's Our Time: Strategic Plan 2003–2008," p. 18.

Such is also the case with other innovative learning strategies, such as Chandler-Gilbert's "Learning Communities" program. According to Lois Bartholomew, dean of student services, all Chandler-Gilbert learning communities have a service-learning component. These learning communities are made up of two or more interdisciplinary courses linked by content, theme, or activity. They facilitate the formation of new approaches to course material and creative interconnections between subjects. The courses, often team-taught, help to "build a sense of community among students and faculty" (Chandler-Gilbert website). Programs that combine multiple alternative pedagogies, such as service-learning and learning communities, profit from the fact that faculty members already involved in one teaching and learning innovation are more likely to be open to trying other, related strategies.

Workforce development and service-learning programs can maximize their effectiveness by acting cooperatively.

Pedagogy and Epistemology

Best Practices

- Integrate service with academics—make it an integral part of course design.
- Ensure that credit is for learning outcomes, not good deeds.
- Define academic outcomes to include all relevant outcomes, including community and workforce development outcomes.
- Give students latitude in choosing projects and project locations.
- Offer reflection activities to deepen learning.
- Find concrete ways to involve the community in the teaching and learning process.

THE INDICATORS DEFINED: PEDAGOGY AND EPISTEMOLOGY

- Community-based work provides an opportunity for students to generate knowledge, develop critical thinking skills, and grapple with the ambiguity of social problems.
- Community knowledge and community expertise are valued as essential to the education of engaged citizens and are incorporated in various ways throughout the curriculum.
- Experiential learning is valued both by faculty and by administrators as an academically credible method of creating meaning and understanding.
- High-level administrators include service-learning in their strategic plans for enhanced academic learning.
- Students are formally introduced to the concepts and skills necessary for community-based work early on in their academic careers.

The Indicators in Action

Although colleges like Raritan Valley—those that have already achieved a critical mass of faculty participants—can realistically identify "nurtur[ing] curricular networks of service-learning and active citizenship" (noted in the college's service-learning brochure) as a way to take their program to the next level, most of the examples of quality service-learning work we found were single courses not connected in any larger educational design. This is not surprising, given the fact that implementing a quality service-learning course requires additional work for most faculty, and creating larger educational units would entail adding still another level of coordination and effort.

Furthermore, the context within which service-learning must operate at most community colleges includes special challenges for both faculty and students. Effectively addressing those challenges implies tailoring established "principles of good practice" in service-learning to a community college environment, and this, in turn, results in a somewhat different typical course profile than one finds at many four-year institutions.

For example, at all the schools we looked at, service-learning is offered far more frequently as an option than as a requirement. At schools like Brevard and Raritan Valley, where a large proportion of the faculty regularly use service-learning, the vast majority do so by offering their students opportunities to choose a community-based assignment either in lieu of some other, more traditional assignment, or as a way to earn additional credit. In describing his program's evolution and operation, Roger Henry, director of Brevard's Center for Service-Learning, identifies the following examples as typical:

> ...an algebra instructor ties 15% of a student's grade for the course to its service-learning component. The only way a student can replace a test score is to successfully document 20 hours of service-learning tutoring in a local high school or on campus, and to write a journal relating that work to course concepts. A developmental psychology instructor automatically increases a student's grade one letter if he/she does 20 hours of service and writes a journal and final essay on the service experience.

This kind of arrangement entails intrinsic benefits as well as intrinsic challenges. On the one hand, it means students who are struggling to find time to attend college in the first place will not have to negotiate still another set of scheduling demands if they don't want to. Those who do choose to participate will bring to their community work the interest and goodwill that attend personal choice.

On the other hand, service-learning as an option runs the risk of marginalizing community work in the context of a course: all students must meet certain "core" academic requirements, but community-based work is not one of them. Hence, for such work to retain its academic credibility, faculty, and those that assist them, must pay special attention to the nature of the connection between the course objective and the service activity. Students must clearly understand that the credit they hope to earn depends upon their ability to demonstrate appropriate learning outcomes, not on having performed "good deeds."

All the more advanced programs we looked at repeatedly stress integration of service with academic study as one of their most important tasks.

Hence, all the more advanced programs we looked at repeatedly stress integration of service with academic study as one of their most important tasks. At Raritan Valley the chief academic officer, Marie Gnage, made it clear that what she wants is "service-learning as an integral part of course design, not as an added element." Similarly, one of the deans at Chandler-Gilbert explained, "In our model, the teacher has to be completely connected. [There] are obligations for each participant, [including] critical connections to the course material." At Albuquerque TVI, some community partners reported that students brought their syllabi with them so the partners could help them make such connections.

To be sure, we also found considerable latitude among community college personnel in defining what, in fact, constitutes a legitimate course-service connection. For the most part, both the administrators and the faculty we interviewed rejected the idea that mastery of disciplinary content should be the only appropriate measure of student learning. As a group of faculty at Brevard put it, "We want holistic teachers... We are looking for something beyond just knowledge of the content area." The chair of Raritan Valley's nursing department explained it this way: "Service-learning is strong...because faculty see it's about more than learning an academic subject, and this is what it means to teach in a community college." In this she was articulating a widely held sentiment.

It would be difficult to overestimate the importance of this point in identifying the distinctive nature and promise of service-learning as a teaching-learning strategy at community colleges. When Robert Barr and John Tagg (1995), themselves from a community college, made their critical (and widely cited) distinction between college as a place "to provide instruction" and as a place "to produce learning," they implicitly identified a far less restrictive approach to academic legitimacy than is the case at many four-year schools. If service-learning can indeed facilitate the development of valuable skills, expose students to potential role models, increase their overall motivation to learn, and help them better understand "the idea of public good," why would one *not* want to include it in one's repertoire of instructional strategies?

The cogency of this approach is, of course, strongly reinforced by the commitment of community colleges to an open enrollment policy. At Albuquerque TVI, for example, fully 58% of the students test into developmental studies—"These students were never engaged in high school," notes one administrator—and service-learning is seen as one important way to draw them in. The story at Malcolm X is similar: the role the college plays in the community compels it to see itself as a "bridging institution," making up for inadequate high schools. For colleges that must play this role, a narrow understanding of academic relevance may be more than just a little irrelevant. It is interesting to note that at Miami Dade's Engaged Department Institute, one of the academic areas best represented was college preparation.

Whether or not experiential learning strategies such as service-learning must operate in the context of underserved populations, they can often serve to generate stronger student motivation and deeper engagement with course material. As Margaret West, an English instructor at Anne Arundel, observed, the required service-learning component in her basic writing course "gets [students] involved in the course and gives them something to write about and something to care about. [It generates] emotional involvement."

Furthermore, the fact that most community colleges have a strong commitment to workforce development may itself lead to a more flexible understanding of what "counts" as academically relevant. In our conversations with students from Raritan Valley and Chandler-Gilbert, schools with constituencies more suburban than urban, we repeatedly found a coupling of academic, community/civic, and workforce considerations. For example, almost all the Raritan Valley students cited in the college's service-learning brochure seamlessly link community experiences to personal career goals. The following is typical: "Community service programs like service-learning not only enlightened my values and perceptions, it [sic] changed my career choice. Since leaving Raritan Valley Community College, I enrolled in the social work program at Rutgers University."

For such students, it is literally "academic" to attempt to distinguish "pure" learning from vocational experiences or civic awareness. Service-learning allows them to expand their sense of what is personally, professionally, and socially possible, and they show little inclination to separate these spheres into water-tight compartments. Administrators often make the same point. "There exist at Kapi'olani in general organic connections among the various components and constituencies," one administrator told us. The same culture that led the college to integrate student affairs counselors directly into academic content areas also leads to a constant blending of academic, workforce, and community outcomes. The result is demonstrated excellence in all three areas.

One concrete example of such blending can be found in Southern Maine Community College's Fire Science program, which provides students with an opportunity to participate as live-in members of local fire departments. Several towns surrounding the college open their firehouses to Fire Science students, providing them with invaluable on-the-job training while they themselves benefit from the additional manpower. One student in the program noted proudly that Southern Maine Community College participants receive special "fire department" shirts, signifying their membership in the group.

According to Mike McGovern, town manager of Cape Elizabeth, Maine, these students add considerably to the community's emergency response capability. The value the community places on these services is evident in its construction of a new firehouse in Cape Elizabeth. As McGovern explained, "One important fact that we made sure we considered when we were building our new fire station in town was the addition of extra rooms for students. We wanted to be a part of the In House Fire Program, and the community included extra rooms so this could happen."

Hocking College in Ohio provides another excellent example of the blending of academic, workforce, and community concerns. There an Environmental Restoration program helps retrain the area's many unemployed miners to restore abandoned mine sites. According to Elaine Dabelko, Hocking's Associate Vice President for Academic Affairs:

> As the ex-miners learn to use heavy earth-moving equipment in the restoration projects, they reflect on the consequences of mining activities and in the process become highly employable. The program's job placement record is very good. It is an excellent model of service-learning and workforce development integration.... The program serves as an on-campus model as well, and curricular integration is now required...by the board of trustees. The college asks that students demonstrate community and cultural engagement as one of its required general skills.

"Most instructors leave the students a lot of room to choose and shape their community project."

Although the college originally approached service-learning in a manner described by one administrator as "too rigid"—as something unto itself—those involved quickly learned that integration was the key to success.

Finally, the fact that most community college students are commuters with numerous non-academic obligations demands not only that they have a choice as to whether to participate in service-learning but also that they be able to choose a project literally and figuratively "close to home." As a student at Raritan Valley noted, "Most instructors leave the students a lot of room to choose and shape their community project." This, in turn, made it "more likely they would find a project of personal interest." Such logistical flexibility, however, often requires a corresponding conceptual flexibility. Faculty need to be willing to consider a variety of ways in which service work can legitimately advance course objectives.

All of this is not to imply that "anything goes." As Brevard's Roger Henry notes: "The [Center for Service-Learning] promulgates basic guidelines and minimum standards to ensure an academic-community balance." Similarly, Anne Arundel Community

College has recently developed a new reflection and assessment series entitled "Let's Talk Assessment." According to Casey-Whiteman, service-learning "comes up a lot at these meetings," and involved faculty are asked to give clear examples demonstrating how student learning is furthered by their courses' service-learning component. Nonetheless, community college instructors enjoy—and demonstrate—considerable flexibility in determining what students can do to meet course requirements. Perhaps the one constant we found emphasized across the board was the fundamental importance of reflection in turning "raw experience" into genuine learning. In the words of Miami Dade President Eduardo Padrón, "the most important aspect of a service-learning course is the reflection component."

In the words of Miami Dade President Eduardo Padrón, "the most important aspect of a service-learning course is the reflection component."

The actual reflection strategies community colleges employ do not necessarily differ from those employed at other kinds of institutions. Centers like the one at Miami Dade provide numerous opportunities for faculty to learn reflection-related skills and techniques. In some cases, partners provide supplemental reflection opportunities of their own. At schools like Albuquerque TVI and Chandler-Gilbert, campus-wide reflection sessions are held every semester.

Especially interesting in this regard are campus-wide reflection opportunities organized around community and civic engagement as valuable activities in themselves. Brevard, for example, offers a special 3-credit course in community involvement, while Miami Dade sponsors a Forum on Civic Responsibility. At some schools, civic reflection is supported primarily through events that focus on specific community issues.

Most community colleges committed to civic engagement make community-based work a central teaching and learning strategy. A central question, then, is to what extent do their community partners actually help shape the teaching/learning process? Clearly, community partners are highly valued, as are the experiences and the skills development they make possible. In addition, they often provide respected mentors for students who are considering careers in related fields. All of this should not be underestimated, especially given the thinly disguised disdain for practitioners that often prevails in other sectors of higher education.

Still, for the most part we did not find that community partners had the kind of regular, substantive contact with faculty that would allow them to play a genuinely shaping role in the educational process. As Brevard's Roger Henry noted:

> While a major strength of Brevard's program is its central coordination, this strength is also a weakness because faculty frequently depend on the [Center for Service-Learning] for too much. Some instructors do not have or make the time to be involved outside of their regular courses.

In other words, when it comes to civic engagement, few structures exist that are comparable to the workforce advisory councils that seek to involve relevant and knowledgeable non-academics in the design of the learning process. At their best such councils can help guide curriculum and program development in ways consistent with real-world needs and interests, and can help establish meaningful measures of practice.

To be sure, some community partners do play an active role in facilitating reflection, and such facilitation could provide an opening for greater faculty-partner collaboration. Perhaps the chief academic officer at Raritan Valley, Marie Gnage, said it best when she observed that:

> Among the many things community-based organizations have to teach are (1) the importance of civic involvement and the kinds of contributions individuals can make; (2) the limited resources many community-based organizations have to deal with; (3) how issues are advanced in the "real" world; and (4) course-related knowledge.

Their potential to deliver on this educational promise has yet to be fully realized. One reason is that many community organizations lack the time and resources to devote much of either to curricular issues. Providing structures for involvement that take these issues into account (e.g., one-hour monthly sessions held on-site) can increase efficiency and make the process more appealing for community partners. For a lengthier, more involved commitment, it may be helpful to offer some form of compensation.

Faculty Culture

Closely related to curricular issues are issues of faculty culture. If faculty feel neither prepared nor rewarded for their engaged work, the curricular connection cannot long survive. In this chapter we look at how faculty culture can foster engagement—specifically, we examine those indicators that suggest faculty are receiving the support they need if they are to assume the task of linking the curriculum to the community.

Faculty Development

Best Practices

- Centralize faculty development resources and build engagement into development efforts.
- Create a culture of service through hiring and buy-in from key academic administrators.
- Provide on-campus training and incentives for participation.
- Actively recruit adjunct faculty to participate in community-related activities.
- Seek external funding to support engagement efforts.
- Document results to justify resource allocation.

THE INDICATORS DEFINED: FACULTY DEVELOPMENT

- The college regularly provides faculty with in-house opportunities to become familiar with teaching methods and practices related to service-learning.
- Mechanisms have been developed to help faculty mentor and support each other in learning to design and implement service-learning courses.
- To enhance their ability to offer quality service-learning courses, faculty have access to curriculum development grants, reductions in teaching loads, and/or travel grants to attend regional and national conferences focused on engaged work.

The Indicators in Action

Among the colleges we looked at, we found significant differences in the degree to which general enthusiasm for faculty civic and community engagement among administrators translates into specific development programs and opportunities. Among those schools that do take faculty development seriously there seem to be three general approaches.

The first approach is organized around a centralized development plan that all faculty are expected to follow. Service-learning and/or civic engagement is just one of many teaching/learning strategies faculty may adopt, but it is often one of the best organized.

An excellent example of this model can be found at Anne Arundel Community College, where all new faculty must participate in a year-long Learning College (LC) supported and run by the Institutional Professional Development office. Each faculty participant receives a course release in his/her first semester, commits to 45 contact hours of LC work during his or her first year, and by June 30 must submit a professional development plan highlighting areas for future work. Service-learning is included in the LC program, and experienced service-learning faculty assist the newcomers. Perhaps not surprisingly, more and more faculty plans now include service-learning. Complementary to this first-year faculty development program is an annual three-day college-wide faculty orientation at the start of the fall semester. Here too service-learning is well represented, with a special seminar repeated throughout the event. Many who adopt service-learning do so after participating in this seminar at the start of their second year.

Anne Arundel Community College also offers a three-part faculty service-learning institute. In part one, faculty participate in discussions of and approaches to service-learning. In part two, they go to an agency to do service on their own for three hours. In part three, they reflect on their community experience and further develop their understanding of community-based work. Faculty who complete all three parts of the institute receive funding to attend the annual conference of the Community College National Center for Community Engagement (CCNCCE). It is not unusual for these faculty to return to campus as real service-learning "cheerleaders." Over time, this strategy has built a strong cadre of faculty committed to deep and increasing involvement in the community.

A second faculty development approach also features centralized resources, but seeks to have an impact less through a set plan than through "saturation." Perhaps the master of this approach is Roger Henry, director of the Center for Service-Learning (CSL) at Brevard Community College, whose ability to recruit faculty one way or another has led college personnel to coin the word "Rogerized."

The CSL regularly offers a wide variety of community-related opportunities, including workshops and courses, immersion events, school partnerships, conferences, and publication opportunities. Central to this approach is a "point system" that determines a faculty member's contract status. (Miami Dade has a very similar system.) By persuading the administration to recognize service-learning activities as a legitimate way of earning points, the CSL has succeeded in giving faculty a very practical reason to take advantage of its offerings. The combination of this faculty incentive, Henry's skill in making one-on-one connections, and the way in which service has come to define the Brevard experience has helped ensure the program's success.

A third development approach shares a pervasive focus on service but grounds that focus less in a well-orchestrated set of opportunities than in a decentralized culture of service as a way of life. Kapi'olani Community College clearly excels at this approach, for despite an absence of many of the formal mechanisms identified above, Kapi'olani faculty express both an understanding of and a commitment to community-based work.

The key to Kapi'olani's success depends in part on the college's hiring practices. Few among the schools we looked at have so succeeded in making hiring policy a vehicle of faculty development. The college has managed to attract and retain a critical mass of faculty who see their own productivity, creativity, and commitment in relation to the greater community. This type of development has been made possible because of the leadership and commitment of the college's chancellor and CAO, John Morton, and the group of deans he has assembled around him. Because this group of administrative/academic leaders agrees on the central role of community engagement at Kapi'olani, they have been highly successful in communicating that priority to both existing and prospective faculty.

What is unusual is the extent to which the culture of engagement has become a defining characteristic of the faculty.

Given this kind of workforce, faculty development at Kapi'olani is more a matter of helping individuals get the intellectual and fiscal resources they need to do their community-related work than of setting up opportunities to get faculty on board. To be sure, the actual faculty development resources the school makes available—workshops, mini-grants, publications, conference travel—are not all that different from what we found elsewhere. What is unusual is the extent to which the culture of engagement has become a defining characteristic of the faculty and their sense of identity.

To what extent such an approach is replicable is an open question. Aside from the disclaimers we heard other administrators express about what is possible vis-à-vis the hiring process, few other schools seem to be able to draw upon the community-oriented cultural attitudes that permeate Kapi'olani and are seen as a natural part of its Polynesian cultural heritage. The only other two schools where something similar seems to prevail are Malcolm X College and Yakima Valley Community College, where a powerful minority culture has helped forge an analogous sense of natural interconnectedness and social responsibility. At Malcolm X, the operative word for the college community is "family," and this self-image carries with it many of the same assumptions and priorities.

However, whether or not a college is positioned to benefit from a community-oriented cultural setting, fostering a sense of institutional belonging is essential for effective faculty development. This is especially true when it comes to the role of adjuncts in a college's service-learning activities.

Fostering a sense of institutional belonging is essential for effective faculty development.

On many campuses, adjunct faculty feel marginalized and excluded from professional development opportunities. Brevard Community College is one college that is seeking to "mend the rift with adjuncts," as one faculty member put it. At Brevard, adjuncts are explicitly encouraged to come to development workshops and are assigned a formal partnership with a full-time faculty member. Many of these partnerships develop into longer, productive relationships. Portland Community College also seeks to avoid a rift with its adjuncts by deliberately pursuing and encouraging their participation in service-learning activities. In a letter to all part-time faculty members, Service-Learning Faculty Coordinator Kim Smith acknowledges that part-time faculty "may feel sometimes like you are less integrated into the college community than you would like" and stresses that "one way to be more connected to the college and the community is through service-learning." The letter goes on to list the substantial number of campus resources readily available to full- and part-time faculty alike (see the boxed insert on the next page).

Turning now to what most successful faculty development efforts have in common, we can identify several broad areas of agreement. As noted earlier, the resources made available to faculty do not differ greatly across the institutions we examined. More or less standard are (1) on-campus training opportunities; (2) publications, course models, and exemplary syllabi; (3) opportunities for community immersion experiences and faculty experiential learning; and (4) opportunities to attend local, regional, and national conferences. Many schools also offer incentives such as a reduced course load (for new courses or new faculty) and mini-grants.

Less ubiquitous but still relatively common are faculty-faculty mentoring arrangements. In the Chandler-Gilbert model, the college has created "service-learning faculty liaisons"—individuals who are knowledgeable, experienced, and well-positioned to help with service-learning activities. Their fellow faculty members know them as the people to go to for information and support. For this program, the college budgets for $8,000 of release time per year; some years this amount is awarded to one individual, and other years it is shared among several people. Now in place for more than ten years, this arrangement has become an integral part of the college's service-learning initiative.

In addition to allocating institutional resources for faculty development, many schools have also sought external funding. The American Association of Community Colleges (AACC) in particular has played a critical role in supporting service-learn-

EXAMPLE FROM THE FIELD: LETTER TO PART-TIME FACULTY INVITING COMMUNITY CONNECTION

Dear Faculty,

Welcome to the Part-Time Inservice, from the Service-Learning Steering Committee! As part-time faculty, we know that you do a lot for PCC, yet you also may feel sometimes like you are less integrated into the college community than you would like. Well, one way to be more connected to the college and the community is through service-learning.

The service-learning program at PCC continues to grow, with over 100 faculty incorporating community service and experiential learning into their courses. Service-learning allows faculty, students, and community partners to increase their understanding of social issues and course material by connecting learning objectives and reflection exercises to service in the community. Students rave about the program and we hope that you will consider using service-learning in your courses as well.

There are a number of ways that we can support you in your service-learning efforts.

- Kim Smith, the Service-Learning Faculty Coordinator, provides faculty support in course development, funding, and information resources. She can be reached at...
- Betsy Warriner, the Learn and Serve Project Coordinator, and her assistant Inger Johnson manage our service-learning grant, develop partnerships with schools and community agencies, and promote student volunteerism. For support in finding community partners and service opportunities, contact them at...
- The Cooperative Education offices help support the service-learning program by offering credit for community service and maintaining a database of service opportunities. The database is currently at the Coop office at Sylvania in CC 221, but we hope to have this information available at other campuses and via the web in the near future.
- Resources are available in the library and online at our website http://spot.pcc. edu, as well as through announcements and information sent to the PCC service-learning listserv. Directions for subscribing are available on the website.
- Mini-grants and release-time grants are offered quarterly to support faculty in developing service-learning components in their courses. Note the details in the included flyer.
- And do not forget your fellow faculty. We have service-learning campus representatives on each campus, as well as the many faculty, included on the attached list, who use service-learning in their courses. They have a wealth of information and experience.

We wish you the very best this year at PCC and look forward to working with you! Please feel free to contact us with any questions or comments.

Best wishes,

Kim Smith
Service-Learning Faculty Coordinator

—From Portland Community College

ing faculty development efforts around the country. AACC's national Horizons project (Community Colleges Broadening Horizons through Service-Learning) has provided college personnel with both training and technical assistance, and is itself supported by a grant from the federal government's Corporation for National and Community Service (CNCS). AACC also distributes $3,000 mini-grants to eligible colleges willing to host regional workshops that "focus on aspects of service-learning that are specific to the community college experience." In October 2003 the organization began to distribute a new set of CNCS grants to 10 mentee colleges (that is, those new to service-learning) and to 5 mentor colleges (those experienced in service-learning). Additional faculty development resources come from the Community College National Center for Civic Engagement (CCNCCE), which produces publications, provides training, and helps colleges and community organizations identify and secure funding. But perhaps the best-known contribution CCNCCE has made to faculty development is its annual conference, which is one of the longest-running and most widely attended events in the civic engagement field.

What ultimately justifies faculty development is what such development contributes to demonstrated student success.

Another commonality among successful faculty development activities is their very foundation and defining context; specifically, the way in which they are explicitly grounded in an institutional commitment to teaching and learning. Whether in any given case service-learning is seen as the pedagogy of choice or as just one option among many, what ultimately justifies faculty development is what such development contributes to demonstrated student success. Hence, service-learning as *pedagogy* complements service-learning as *vehicle of civic commitment.*

Finally, we found that the most effective faculty development efforts are able to identify, accommodate, and even co-opt already existing fiscal, organizational, and cultural resources. Rather than waiting for *the* grant that will allow one to move forward, successful programs make expert use of whatever is already at hand. Examples of supporting faculty development by taking advantage of something already on the books rather than waiting for new moneys include the use of the culture of engagement to prompt engaged work by faculty at Kapi'olani, Malcolm X, and Yakima Valley; the inclusion of service-learning in the Learning College for new faculty at Anne Arundel; and the utilization of the employee wellness hour for service activities at Miami Dade.

Faculty Roles and Rewards

Best Practices

- Create the expectation that faculty will engage in community-related work.
- Tie career advancement to participation in community activities in a concrete way.
- Include community work as a component in faculty dossiers and student evaluations.

• Provide informal ways to recognize faculty's community efforts, such as small grants, awards, and celebrations.

THE INDICATORS DEFINED: FACULTY ROLES AND REWARDS

- The college's tenure, promotion, and/or retention guidelines reflect a range of scholarly activities such as those proposed by Ernest Boyer (1990).
- Faculty data forms, annual reports, and mandatory evaluations all include sections related to civic engagement, professional service, and/or other forms of academically based public work.
- The college explicitly encourages academic departments to include community-based interests and experience as criteria in their faculty recruiting efforts.

The Indicators in Action

As many of the above examples of faculty development suggest, faculty development and faculty recognition often go hand in hand—especially in a community college context, where professional development and contract renewal are directly linked. Unlike the situation that prevails at many four-year institutions, faculty review is not focused on a single, all-important tenure decision, and community college demonstrations of excellence naturally include professional activities as well as professional publications.

Thus, for example, Miami Dade's Center for Community Involvement publishes an impressive brochure in which it describes the many "maintenance of rank" options related to service-learning. (To maintain their rank or make progress to the next level, faculty are required to document their participation in professional development activities.) Here one finds, among the offerings, workshops on "Integrating Service-Learning into the Curriculum," "Incorporating Civic Responsibility into the Curriculum," "Reflection and Service-Learning," and "Assessment and the Service-Learning Component." By deepening their understanding of civic engagement and service-learning, faculty can simultaneously advance their own careers. Miami Dade faculty have called this coupling "perhaps the single most effective strategy" the college has employed to advance service-learning. It was, as one individual put it, "a brilliant stroke."

Community college demonstrations of excellence naturally include professional activities as well as professional publications.

However, not all the schools we looked at link community-related work and faculty recognition in such a seamless way. Far more common than any formal connection is faculty recognition that work of this kind is not just respected, it is *expected,* and meeting this expectation will bring many professional and personal benefits. At Portland Community College, faculty self-assessments demonstrate service activities for contract-related purposes. At Malcolm X, not only are faculty dossiers required to address civic and community work, student course evaluations also include an item that asks whether the instructor has encouraged such work.

At several colleges, including Kapi'olani, Chandler-Gilbert, and Raritan Valley among others, community-based work has become such a deep and pervasive part of faculty culture that the administration hardly needs to stress its importance. Here is John Morton, Chancellor and CAO of Kapi'olani, describing the college's culture:

> To understand how support for civically engaged work evolved, one must first understand the college's history of supporting other institution-wide teaching/learning initiatives.... Well before service-learning, broad responsibilities had become a hallmark of Kapi'olani faculty in several areas, including diversity and IT....
>
> There is palpable faculty peer pressure to do civically engaged work: excellence in this area sets the institutional tone, and this in turn results in a difference in faculty productivity, creativity, and commitment.

But regardless of the various ways in which the schools we looked at articulate a link between civic engagement and institutional expectations, they all have managed to implement effective and creative ways of recognizing faculty efforts. For in addition to the more or less formal ways in which such efforts are tied to promotion, tenure, and professional advancement, a host of other, more individual mechanisms exist to let faculty know their work is appreciated. At Brevard, for example, faculty can apply for special Voluntary Incentive Program (VIP) grants, basing their applications on their community-related work. An award means an additional $1,250 added to the applicant's base salary.

At Collin County Community College District outside of Dallas, monetary awards take a different form. Here the president awards student scholarships for service-learning participation in the name of faculty and staff members who have themselves excelled in community-based work. According to Regina Hughes, director of the college's new Center for Scholarly and Civic Engagement, honorees find this highly creative form of recognition as meaningful as the college finds it economically efficient. Also at Collin County, faculty are eligible to receive study grants of $2,500—or can apply for a sabbatical—on the basis of their service-learning, civic engagement, or other professional development interests.

Not all community colleges have the resources to make special monetary awards, but all have the capacity to bestow public praise. President Zerrie Campbell of Malcolm X notes that "recognition and rewards seem to be very important to faculty"; her faculty in turn appreciate her attention to this issue and note that she is very effective at "assuaging [their] egos." For example, Malcolm X uses email to consistently recognize faculty and staff, organizes recognition luncheons, nominates faculty for statewide awards, offers its own "distinguished awards" in many employee categories, and has created a "Wall of Fame" where photos of winners are hung. (Portland Community College also posts photos of faculty who have performed outstanding community work.)

Thank you notes from administrators and community partners; articles on faculty work in local newspapers, campus newsletters, and alumni magazines; mention of such work in reports to the board of trustees; letters of support for outside grants and honors—all of these signify that civic and community engagement efforts are both noticed and appreciated on campus. But perhaps the single most frequently used form of public recognition is the special celebratory event. Every year Brevard Community College holds a luncheon for more than 200 people to recognize engaged faculty. The entire administration attends. Raritan Valley and Malcolm X also hold recognition luncheons, and Portland holds awards dinners.

For many faculty, of course, the intrinsic rewards of community work are by far the most important. As Linda Krupp, a faculty member at Brevard, has written of one of her service-learning classes:

> I had the opportunity to witness the transformation of lives during this class.... Through each of these students, I shared the heartaches, tribulations, jubilance, challenges, failures and successes they experienced. My world began to expand beyond the classroom; my own level of social consciousness and awareness was raised.

This sentiment was echoed either explicitly or implicitly in the comments of engaged faculty at virtually every college we visited.

This is, perhaps, not surprising since Campus Compact's annual member survey confirms the importance faculty place on the intrinsic rewards service-learning offers both their students and themselves. To a question concerning factors most effective in motivating faculty to incorporate service and engagement into their teaching and research, one of the most frequent response in each of the past three surveys (2001–2003) was the desire to promote active/engaged learning. Other motivational factors included facilitating student learning of course content, development of critical thinking skills, exposing students to diversity, and development of civic skills and responsibilities.

INTRINSIC REWARDS OF FACULTY ENGAGEMENT

Reasons Faculty Incorporate Community Work into the Curriculum	Rank (out of 5)
Facilitating student learning of course content	4.5
Promoting active/engaged learning	4.4
Development of students' critical thinking skills	4.4
Exposing students to diversity	4.1
Development of civic skills and responsibilities	3.9

—From Campus Compact's annual member survey, 2003

In conclusion, we should stress again that at the colleges we examined most formal vehicles of faculty recognition are not exclusive to service-learning and civic engagement. All good, innovative teaching is supported, and leadership in problem-based learning, development of critical thinking, and other learning goals is also enthusiastically recognized. Brevard's VIP program, Collin County's named scholarship program, and Malcolm X's "Wall of Fame" are not reserved for a single kind of institutional excellence but are available to all who make an outstanding contribution. Nonetheless, the fact that community colleges are indeed "of their communities" makes community-based work, in the words of Brevard's Roger Henry, "a natural" choice for many who seek to excel.

Mechanisms and Resources

Successful engagement depends not only on institutional culture and faculty interest; it also depends—often directly—on the concrete mechanisms and specific resources the college is willing to commit to facilitating the engaged work of faculty and students. This may be especially true at community colleges, where faculty must shoulder some of the heaviest teaching loads in higher education. Furthermore, an institution's commitment to such mechanisms and resources must be sufficiently strong that it can survive the pressures of competing priorities and difficult economic times. In this chapter we look at those indicators that relate to a supportive infrastructure. We also look at the ways in which students themselves support and structure the engagement process.

Enabling Mechanisms

Best Practices

- Create an office of community-based teaching and learning, or incorporate this function into the work of other offices or centers (e.g., student affairs or workforce development).
- Set up a website with information directed toward students, faculty, and community partners—including a database with partnership opportunities.
- Use orientations and classroom visits to inform students and faculty of the importance of civic engagement and of specific activities and services.

THE INDICATORS DEFINED: ENABLING MECHANISMS

- The college maintains a centralized office that is committed to community-based teaching and learning and clearly aligned with academic affairs.
- The college has developed a full range of forms and procedures that allow it to organize and document community-based work.
- Faculty and students are kept well informed of the resources available to support community-based work. These resources are effectively included in all faculty and student orientation programs.
- The college recognizes the unusual demands created by work in the community and attempts to provide flexible scheduling options for faculty and students.
- The college recognizes that course content can be delivered in many ways and allows faculty sufficient freedom to utilize community-based strategies.
- The college recruits and trains student leaders to work with faculty and community partners.

- Use students as central program resources.
- Provide events and opportunities for engagement, such as employee release time and community fairs.

The Indicators in Action

When we speak of "enabling mechanisms" (Walshock 1995), we are referring to a wide variety of structures, procedures, print and electronic resources, events, opportunities, and personnel whose function is to facilitate civic and community engagement on the part of all campus stakeholders. Some of these mechanisms, especially as they apply to faculty, have already been discussed in earlier chapters. Others, especially as they apply to the processing of broad public issues and community concerns, will be discussed in the next chapter. Our focus here is on operational rather than academic resources and is geared more toward bringing the campus to the community than the other way around.

Foremost among these enabling mechanisms are the specific offices many colleges have created to promote and facilitate community-based teaching and learning. Among the schools we looked at, those with strong, developed community engagement programs all have such offices—although schools differ in the degree to which they seek to centralize their support operations.

At schools with more centralized programs, such offices can be impressive in their size and reach. President Eduardo Padrón at Miami Dade College characterizes his own service-learning office as "an internally-funded, college-wide infrastructure that includes three comprehensive 'Centers for Community Involvement,' a district director, three campus coordinators, faculty coordinators, [and] student ambassadors." At Brevard Community College, Center for Service-Learning Director Roger Henry describes a similar operation:

> Resources for CSL [the Center for Service-Learning] are four full-time staff and four part-time staff, eight student workers, and five to six SL Leaders. The college supports the four full-time staff and provides a large office and classroom. We have offices on each campus. The total budget is $332,000, with over $200,000 being general fund monies from the college.

Few operations are as extensive as those at Miami Dade and Brevard. Nevertheless, most developed programs have, at the very least, a full-time director, several office staff (student, full-time, or part-time), a coordinator if the college has multiple campuses, and sufficient office space to allow these individuals to do their work.

Similarly, most developed offices provide a range of services. Among the most important are what Roger Henry (1998, p. 86) has called "tangible tools"; "i.e., program brochures, posters, student application forms, placement process guidelines, a fact sheet, and a directory of service opportunities." Like many of the other programs we looked at, Brevard's CSL creates such tools to meet the particular needs of each of

SELECTED COMMUNITY SERVICE AND SERVICE-LEARNING CENTER WEBSITES

Many community service/service-learning center websites provide useful information for faculty, students, and community agencies wishing to participate in campus/community activities. Such websites often include a list of community agencies, access to the forms required by the college, testimonials about service-learning from campus and community members, links to national resources, and information about the resources produced by the college regarding community-based activities and strategies. Following are the relevant websites of many of the colleges discussed in this monograph.

Albuquerque Technical Vocational Institute
http://planet.tvi.cc.nm.us/servicelearning/index.htm

Brevard Community College
www.brevardcc.edu (click on site map, then choose "Center for Service Learning" under "Student Life")

Chandler-Gilbert Community College
www.cgc.maricopa.edu/service_learning

College of Lake County
www.clcillinois.edu/academics/servicelearn.asp

Collin County Community College District
www.ccccd.edu/servicelearning/index.html

Hocking College
www.hocking.edu/~aaffairs/SVCLNG.HTML

Johnson County Community College
http://old.jccc.net/acad/studserv/career/serv_learn/index.htm

Kapi'olani Community College
www.kcc.hawaii.edu/academics/service/index.htm

Kirtland Community College
http://services.kirtland.edu/servicelearning/default.htm

Malcolm X College
http://malcolmx.ccc.edu/president/default.asp

Miami Dade College
www.mdcc.edu/cci

Middlesex Community College
www.middlesex.cc.ma.us/service-learning/ServiceLearning.htm

Mount Wachusett Community College
www.mwcc.mass.edu/HTML/Report/community.html

Portland Community College
http://spot.pcc.edu/slp/index.html

Raritan Valley Community College
www.raritanval.edu/rvcc/frameset/sitemap.html (click on "Service Learning")

Virginia Highlands Community College
www.vh.cc.va.us/studentdevelopment/Volunteer/Default.htm

its primary constituencies: students, faculty, and community partners. Indeed, creating tangible tools has become something of a Brevard specialty, and its materials have been copied and adopted at dozens of other colleges across the country.

One of the most dynamic and accessible tools colleges use both to promote and to enhance civic engagement activities is a comprehensive, up-to-date program website. The best websites we visited include resources for all the primary constituencies identified above. These resources may include an introduction to campus-based community work and service-learning, instructions on how to become involved, downloadable forms, lists or descriptions of existing partnerships and available partnering opportunities, links to other websites and resources, and campus contact information. Some schools, such as Brevard, allow students to register with the Center for Service-Learning online. Some, like Chandler-Gilbert, provide a page of past students' reflections on their community learning experiences. Raritan Valley also offers a sampling of community partner reflections. Colleges that produce print resources typically provide information about how to purchase or acquire them.

> The importance of a comprehensive, up-to-date, user-friendly database can hardly be overestimated.

Databases of available projects and partnerships cannot, of course, simply be purchased and adapted. Each must be carefully constructed and maintained. Since the kinds of course-community matches available affect not only the quality of the academic learning involved but also the value of the service provided and the ease with which students can accommodate community-based work into their schedules, the importance of a comprehensive, up-to-date, user-friendly database can hardly be overestimated. Anne Arundel Community College has an established procedure that begins this way:

> A faculty member who wants a class project puts in a request. Then we poll agencies to see what's needed—for example, a computer person looking for a project.... Then [possibilities are] sent...back to the faculty member. We [also] keep track of class stories—success stories. Business students working on measuring substandard housing is a new project.... [Plus,] we have "wish lists" for agencies in the database for matching people.

As this example suggests, the uses to which programs put their computerized databases go well beyond facilitating appropriate campus-community matches. Speaking of her work as a service-learning assistant at Chandler-Gilbert, one student enthused that "our database is very sophisticated. [It] sorts information by all sorts of things and can show our history over time. [It] can do more than anyone thought." This "more" includes formatting letters of appreciation and student certificates.

Still another core function of most offices is orienting both faculty and students to the scope of their operations, explaining why community and civic engagement is so important, and indicating how the office staff can meet specific needs. Information of this sort may be provided during the course of general college-wide orientations as well as visits to individual classes. At Albuquerque TVI, where the community program is lodged within student services, staff provide an orientation for all new personnel each semester. Service-learning and civic engagement are introduced to "counselors, advisors, financial aid, assessment, [and] health center staff." At many schools, core program staff, community partners, and specially trained students take turns visiting classes where community-based work is either an option or a requirement.

Using students as a program resource seems to be an idea whose time has come. For much of the last decade, colleges and national organizations have expended considerable time and energy in exploring the faculty role in building campus-community partnerships. Far less attention has been given to the student role in such foundational work. For the most part, students have been seen as program beneficiaries, not as program leaders. When they have been included as staff, more often than not their function has been limited to office work paid through work-study.

Increasingly, however, student interest, experience, and expertise are being seen as invaluable program resources. Not only can students file and answer the phone, they introduce other students to the why's and how's of community-based work. They can also assist faculty in making and sustaining community connections, and in leading reflection sessions and assessing outcomes. As "site supervisors" they can serve as the college's eyes and ears at a community location and as the community's advocates on campus. Through such responsibilities they can not only further their own personal development; they can also make it possible for a program to have a degree of staff "coverage" it could otherwise not afford. Miami Dade's "Ambassadors," Brevard's "Service-Learning Leaders," Chandler-Gilbert's "Service-Learning Assistants"—all enable both faculty members and community partners to receive individualized attention.

Increasingly, student interest, experience, and expertise are being seen as invaluable program resources.

Although specialized offices represent the most common—and from the standpoint of the curriculum, possibly the most important—enabling mechanism colleges have developed to facilitate community and civic engagement, they are by no means the only mechanism. Several of the colleges we looked at have created other kinds of bridges to the wider community. At Albuquerque TVI, for example, a new Southwest Center for Environmental Excellence and Opportunity seeks to

> Improve Hispanic participation in U.S. Department of Energy (DOE) environmental clean-up activities and encourage Hispanics to pursue educational and career opportunities in engineering science and new technologies in a culturally and linguistically appropriate manner.

Thus, like the Hocking College project described in an earlier chapter, the Southwest Center combines civic, academic, and workforce-related concerns in a single operation.

At Virginia Highlands Community College in Abingdon, VA, workforce concerns have an office of their own. The Center for Business and Industry (CBI) offers "classes and training programs to meet the needs of individuals and organization within the service region." The center's mission explicitly grounds its work in an ethos of community betterment and local economic development. Community service activities are included in the CBI program as well.

Raritan Valley boasts two centers to complement its service-learning program: The Institute of Holocaust and Genocide Studies Center and The Paul Robeson Institute of Ethics, Leadership, and Social Justice. These three operations are seen as central to the success of one of the college's new strategic initiatives; namely, "Civic

Engagement and Service." Together they make it possible for Raritan Valley students to learn "not only the skills needed to engage in a fulfilling career, but also to have the desire to improve their communities and be active participants in the democratic process."

To be sure, centers are not the only means to advance this goal. Chandler-Gilbert's "Into the Streets" day, like the special outreach events at other community colleges, provides an opportunity for the entire campus to come together around the idea of community engagement. Community fairs, where representatives of local social service, environmental, and other agencies set up informational booths on campus, represent another such opportunity. From the creative use of class scheduling (Chandler-Gilbert) to the extension of employee "wellness" time to include community service activities (Brevard), community colleges have effectively appropriated whatever was available to make civic and community engagement a signature part of their identity.

Internal Resource Allocation

Best Practices

- Make engagement a fiscal priority by acknowledging its importance as a teaching tool and including it in the college's strategic plan.
- Ally with staff development and other existing functions to create efficiencies.
- Create "marketing" materials to publicize the college's community work.
- Provide sufficient office space for community and service-learning coordination efforts.

The Indicators in Action

Almost everything discussed in the last three chapters is predicated upon a willingness to make civic and community engagement a fiscal as well as a rhetorical priority. In times of financial hardship this requires tremendous commitment—remember President Eduardo Padrón's observation that, at an institution that had lost 300 positions since 1996, "It would have been easy to eliminate service-learning." Difficult as it is to maintain this level of commitment, to reap the full benefits of campus engagement—academic, workforce

THE INDICATORS DEFINED: INTERNAL RESOURCE ALLOCATION

- Adequate funding is provided to support, enhance, and deepen involvement by faculty, students, and staff in community-based work.
- The college regularly draws upon already existing resources to strengthen engagement activities. Such activities are seen as priorities in the allocation of those resources.
- The college provides sufficient long-term staffing for all core partnerships and engagement activities. It also provides adequate office space for that staff to do its work.

development, and community—service-learning and engagement efforts must be sustainable.

That said, the creativity and energy required to develop effective enabling mechanisms and the conviction and commitment required to institutionalize those mechanisms are two very different things. Among the schools we looked at, some that have done well with the first task still have a way to go with the second. In the meantime, they are improvising with soft money and a few extraordinary individuals.

Because service-learning and civic engagement contribute little directly to an institution's bottom line, adequate internal resources can be guaranteed only if the institution sees them as central to its identity. This is the real significance of President Padrón's follow-up observation that service-learning "has become part of [Miami Dade's] strategic plan," and is now "the essence of the institution."

This is the same message we heard at other colleges where resource allocation has been established on a firm footing. As the preamble to Raritan Valley's new strategic plan puts it:

> The Strategic Plan is intended to highlight the major challenges and opportunities that Raritan Valley Community College faces. It is a document that will help focus and prioritize monetary expenditures on goals that will add value to the College.

Thus, Chief Academic Officer Marie Gnage believes the adoption of the plan can be considered a "watershed event in the school's history. Through the explicit emphasis it places on civic engagement, it will anchor all future decisions regarding the prioritization of scarce resources."

At Anne Arundel, the college's ability to make a strong financial commitment to engagement depends, above all, on its conviction that cutting support for the Office of Service-Learning would significantly affect quality teaching and learning. If the budget must be cut, it must be cut only in accordance with "mission mandates" and an explicit set of "guiding principles." If quality learning represents an essential "service," service-learning is not the place to look for cost-saving measures.

Collaboration is far more appropriate than competition—and costs a lot less.

Anne Arundel also demonstrates another important aspect of effective internal resource allocation; namely, maximum utilization of existing opportunities. As noted in the discussion of effective faculty development strategies, opportunism can be a virtue when linked to a good cause. The way in which Anne Arundel has taken advantage of the Learning College (LC), supported and run by its Institutional Professional Development Office, is a case in point. Given the existence of such a well-designed and well-respected faculty training program, collaboration is far more appropriate than competition—and costs a lot less. Brevard has been similarly creative in linking service-learning with existing structures. It is this strategy that has led the Center for Service-Learning to ally with nearly every staff development initiative the college offers.

Perhaps a special word needs to be said about another internal resource not directly related to budget: creative marketing or publicizing an institution's commitment to community engagement. Anne Arundel provides a noteworthy model, having developed a range of artifacts that serve as an effective way to support faculty service-learning efforts and to create an environment that affirms civic engagement. Visitors to the college find paper cubes containing service-learning information, mouse pads listing college competencies, and well-distributed brochures highlighting the college's strategic plan. Other schools have used similar strategies to get the word out. Malcolm X deliberately places its namesake's vision of "education for empowerment" on surfaces throughout the campus. Southern Maine Community College has created T-shirts that announce the wearers' participation in the Live-in Firehouse Program. Mugs, magnets, pins, T-shirts, and other materials advertising both the college and its service programs were very much in evidence at most of the campuses we visited.

EXAMPLE FROM THE FIELD: NEW STUDENT CENTER DESCRIPTION

Construction is well underway on the new CGCC Student Center, located on the northwest side of the Pecos Campus.

A large student pavilion will be the focal point of the 20,000 square foot Student Center, providing a gathering space for students and featuring seating for 250. A unique feature of the Student Center is its overhead coiling or "garage doors." When the doors are open, they will allow the pavilion and outside plaza to become one large space for student events or gatherings.

The Student Center will include office space for several Student Services departments, including Counseling Services, Disability Resources and Services, Recruitment, Student Life, Athletics, and the Dean of Student Services office. In addition, the Student Center will house an employee lounge and conference room.

The Student Center, which is scheduled to be completed in early 2003, was awarded an architectural design award by the American Institute of Architects in 2001.

—*From Chandler-Gilbert Community College, September 2002*

Finally, there is that resource called "space." An effective community service or service-learning program needs the practical and psychological security that sufficient office space provides. Not only does it need space, it needs space that is strategically located. Where a college physically situates its partnering efforts can be as revealing as the way in which it prioritizes its budget. In this regard one of the most impressive examples we found of institutional commitment was at Chandler-Gilbert, where service-learning is housed in a new student center designed to promote constant exchange among the college's signature initiatives. Such an arrangement leads directly to our next indicator.

Integrated and Complementary Engagement Activities

Best Practices

- Locate program space centrally to allow maximum collaboration among initiatives.
- Create developmental programs to recruit student leaders.
- Link student affairs, academic affairs, and financial aid through programs that focus on compensated or uncompensated student leadership development.

- Facilitate campus-community communication through publications, information packets, and workshops.

THE INDICATORS DEFINED: INTEGRATED AND COMPLEMENTARY ENGAGEMENT ACTIVITIES

- The college effectively coordinates engagement and service-related activities across academic, co-curricular, and non-academic programs.
- The college makes it possible for community partners to understand, access, and easily navigate the full range of its engagement activities.

The Indicators in Action

Like the effective utilization of existing programs, the effective integration of engagement activities requires vision and imagination more than it does new funds. To continue with Chandler-Gilbert's new student center as an example, the fact that the college had the foresight to recognize that regular interaction between academic and non-academic initiatives could bring about new forms of collaboration has given a boost to its partnering efforts. The college had always seen its various community initiatives as, ideally, both complementary and developmental, but having shared meeting space has helped make this ideal more of a reality.

The effective integration of engagement activities requires vision and imagination more than it does new funds.

"Into the Streets" is a regularly scheduled Chandler-Gilbert event intended to mobilize the entire college—students, faculty, professional and support staff, and administrators—to work in the community at the same time. It is both a morale builder and a very visible demonstration of the college's community orientation. It also serves as the first rung on a developmental ladder.

Although well-designed developmental programs that focus on community and civic engagement are still relatively rare—requiring as they do both a critical mass of activities and the ability to link those activities in a progressive learning sequence—we did find examples of such programming at a few colleges. At Chandler-Gilbert, for example, the "Into the Streets" initiative, among its other functions, provides a valuable opportunity to identify and recruit student leaders. Students can participate in the event either on their own or as part of a class. If such work strikes a particularly responsive chord in them, they can then apply to become "service-learning assistants," coordinating service projects for a particular class. Service-learning assistants work 15 to 20 hours per semester and receive a $100 scholarship. Assistants are responsible for, among other things, data entry tasks and helping with the tracking of service-learning students.

Arrangements like this naturally link student affairs, student leadership, academic affairs, and financial aid. At Chandler Gilbert, club projects (community service) can easily become course-related projects (service-learning), and both can become venues for compensated or uncompensated student leadership development. At Brevard, the broad array of service opportunities open to students finds its most visible manifestation in SHOAT—Service Hours On Academic Transcript. Through the SHOAT program, students can graduate with a comprehensive record of the various service

EXAMPLE FROM THE FIELD: RECORDING ACADEMIC CREDIT FOR SERVICE-LEARNING

Service Hours on Academic Transcript (SHOAT) Guidelines

1. *Enroll:* Complete a Community Service-Learning Application. Visit the Center for Service-Learning, which is conveniently located on each campus.
2. *Verify:* Obtain a Community Service-Learning Hour Report and SHOAT Verification Form. Signature verification must be obtained from the agency supervisor or volunteer coordinator for each service activity.
3. *Return:* The Verification Form must be returned to the Center by the week before final examinations each academic semester.

Service Activities to Be Considered for SHOAT

- Brevard Community College-sponsored service projects that meet a community need both for credit and non-credit (this includes service performed in service-learning courses, in internships with nonprofit or state agencies, and in Service-Learning Clubs, e.g., Rotaract, AASU, etc., that meets a community need).
- Service sponsored by a community service agency, including direct student involvement with local public service agencies.
- Church-sponsored service work where the goal is meeting secular needs (not proselytizing new members); includes assisting at a church soup kitchen or shelter for the homeless.
- Government-sponsored service work (federal, state, and local), including the AmeriCorps Program at the federal level, conservation corps at the state level, and municipal programs such as serving in the school system.
- Independent service projects not sponsored by any agency in areas where legitimate human needs exist but no service agency exists or is equipped to meet those needs.

—*From Brevard Community College (excerpt)*

initiatives in which they participated: not just course-based service-learning but campus club activity, volunteer work, and even student government hours. Furthermore, students whose off-campus service work totals 300 hours or more become eligible to receive a special "Citizen Scholar" designation at graduation.

Mechanisms like these both facilitate and reflect a broader institutional commitment to overcome the compartmentalization so common at higher education institutions. At Kapi'olani, where community service, service-learning, and student leadership blend in much the same way, the administrative leadership long since decided to integrate student affairs counselors directly into academic content areas. This, of course, immediately led to new opportunities for student affairs-faculty affairs collaboration. The integration of civic and community engagement initiatives across administrative boundaries merely reflects a broader arrangement in which such engagement itself complements other cross-college programs like writing across the curriculum and multiculturalism.

One other integrative mechanism deserves to be mentioned: the ways in which community colleges make it easy for their off-campus partners to understand, access, and navigate the full range of campus-based engagement activities. Like civic and community engagement integrated into a developmental sequence, the effective initiation of community partners into a campus's overall civic design (as distinct from communication about specific projects) is still quite rare.

Perhaps the only resources we found widely used in regard to such campus-community communication are the special publications some programs have created to introduce community partners to their work. Brevard makes available to its community partners packets that provide an introduction to utilizing service-learning volunteers, including tips, strategies, pertinent forms, and information on the Center for Service-Learning. Brevard also publishes for its agencies a guide called "Supervisor as Educator" to help them work with service-learning students. This guide contains sections on service-learning definitions, effective utilization of students, orientation and training, student supervision and evaluation, checklists, and sample forms and reports.

Miami Dade goes still further, offering an introductory workshop for its community partners in addition to published material. This workshop covers topics such as the rationale for service-learning, the role of community sites/agencies in higher education and democracy, and the role of reflection activities. It typically includes open discussions regarding challenges, solutions, and next steps.

Student Voice

Best Practices

- Provide opportunities for students to participate as equal members on governance committees and advisory councils.
- Have administrators attend student government meetings to hear and respond to students' ideas and concerns.
- Encourage formal democratic participation such as meetings with state representatives about issues of importance to students.
- Facilitate direct student activism and engagement in social and political issues.

THE INDICATORS DEFINED: STUDENT VOICE

- Students participate on major institutional committees including those that make personnel decisions.
- The college recognizes student-initiated advocacy campaigns as legitimate forms of democratic practice.

The Indicators in Action

We have already discussed at least one of the ways in which community colleges recognize students themselves as an important resource in the area of community and civic engagement. Utilization of students as faculty assistants, site supervisors, and student service mentors helps enlarge the student role from participant to leader, from worker to designer. Elsewhere we have also noted the way in which some colleges (for example, Malcolm X) explicitly ask their students for feedback on the community/civic dimension of their coursework.

One way colleges foster student voice and leadership is to create targeted scholarship opportunities for students who have excelled in community-related work. At Brevard Community College, this takes the form of $500 annual tuition scholarships for service-learning leaders. Responsibilities of the service-learning leaders include recruiting, training, and supervising other students; consulting with service-learning and community agency staff on program design and evaluation; and completing project action plans and reports.

However, as we have repeatedly emphasized, service-learning should ideally be imbedded in a comprehensive culture of service, and such a culture should pay significant attention to student voice in all its forms. More often than not, that voice extends beyond service-learning activities in the technical sense. Many of the schools that boast impressive service-learning programs (and some that do not) also have active student-run groups that are oriented toward community work and civic engagement with little or no academic connection. Such groups can serve as valuable community resources, open significant avenues of engagement, and provide students with powerful opportunities to speak out on public issues.

A growing body of research suggests that many college students view service as an alternative form of democratic participation.

Although both service-learning and non-curricular community service are currently enjoying high levels of popularity among college students, more traditional forms of civic engagement have at the same time experienced a decline, as evidenced by all-time low voting rates among young people. A growing body of research suggests that many college students view service as an alternative form of democratic participation. While on the one hand, such a perspective can be seen as creative and proactive, on the other hand, it remains clear that service complements rather than replaces other forms of civic engagement.

There are, in short, multiple ways in which student voice can manifest itself as an indicator of a school's civic engagement. For example, how seriously does a college take the student role in institutional governance? Shouldn't students being educated to participate actively in our democracy also have a significant say in the running of their own schools?

At Virginia Highlands Community College, not only do three students sit on the President's Advisory Council, the school also places students on all of its standing committees. Thus the students may weigh in on a variety of issues, ranging from student activities (including service activities) to personnel decisions. The Student Government Association (SGA), in turn, facilitates and encourages input by the wider student body in the form of town meetings that are held twice every semester. These meetings are announced well ahead of time, and presided over by the SGA president. A direct link from the Virginia Highlands student webpage makes it easy for students to contact the SGA president with questions or concerns. The fact that the college's vice president for academic affairs is often in attendance allows the administration to hear and respond to students directly.

At Southern Maine Community College, an institution at an early stage in developing its service-learning program, the college has already made a major change in its bylaws. As of September 2002, all college committees include a voting student member. Representatives can be nominated by the student government or by faculty, and serve for a one-year term. In explaining the logic of this new inclusive committee arrangement, the college notes that it

> bases its democratic governance system on the principle that everyone associated with the College must be treated with respect and provided opportunity to express their views on items under consideration.

While the Southern Maine Forum allows students to express their views, formal inclusion of students in the governance system takes the commitment to student voice further by helping to ensure that those views carry some weight.

A similar arrangement can be found at Yakima Valley Community College in central Washington. As at Southern Maine, students at Yakima Valley participate as voting members on important institutional committees, including those concerned with curriculum, hiring, and tenure. They also give regular reports to the board of trustees and participate in decisions that shape important college initiatives, such as the development of a new childcare center.

Indeed, at Yakima Valley, such active democratic practice not only pervades the entire institution on all levels—from student clubs through student government to institutional governance and the allocation of college resources—it also naturally carries over into active democratic practice on a state level. Each year a group of students makes its way to Olympia, the state capital, where the students meet with representatives about issues of concern such as the impact of tuition increases. In short, Yakima Valley's culture of democratic practice goes far beyond the kind of "practice" democracy that is reserved for students at most colleges. In its potential to develop experienced change agents, student participation in governance represents a critically important institutional strategy.

In its potential to develop experienced change agents, student participation in governance represents a critically important institutional strategy.

Encouraging formal democratic participation on and off-campus is undoubtedly a very important way of promoting civic engagement, but democratic practice can also entail a still broader spectrum of activities. Beyond encouraging student involvement in democratic government, community service, and service-learning activities, colleges can also facilitate direct social and political activism and organizing. (For more information, as well as tools to help with such efforts, see Campus Compact's "Raise Your Voice: Student Action for Change" website, www.actionforchange.org.)

Student activism has long been the domain of four-year colleges and universities, a trend caused largely by the unique challenges facing students at two-year institutions—challenges such as shorter enrollment periods and schedules filled with work and family-related obligations. Direct activism is, however, still a viable option at the community college level. Some schools recognize the potential of this form of engagement and have taken active measures to increase socio-political activism on their campuses. Such was the case at Miami Dade when the college co-sponsored and hosted the Learning from Social Movements Summit. Part of the 2003 Raise Your

Voice "Week of Action" activities, the summit was co-sponsored by the national Campus Compact organization, the Campus Outreach Opportunity League (COOL), Florida Campus Compact, and Miami Dade College. According to conference materials, the summit sought to instill in participants "a stronger sense of how their actions tie into a broader, historical framework of people, especially students and young people, working for positive social change." Miami Dade financed the attendance of 80 of its own students, providing them with an important opportunity that otherwise might not have been available.

Collin County Community College District also participated in the Week of Action with a series of on-campus civic events. The week's activities culminated in a day at the Texas Statehouse during which students met with their legislators to discuss a resolution supporting student civic engagement. Like Yakima Valley, Collin County gives its students the opportunity to participate substantively in the democratic process and to do so through multiple forms of engagement.

Community-Campus Exchange

Since the core activity of any college is teaching and learning, we have paid particularly careful attention to the ways in which community colleges have linked civic and community engagement to their curriculum—to what and how their faculty teach and their students learn. However, many of the important civic engagement activities at a community college take place outside of the formal curriculum. As Middlesex Community College's President Carole Cowan succinctly put it, her school's mission is "to teach and to reach."

In this chapter we look at some of the more significant extracurricular ways in which community colleges reach out to their communities: How they make resources available to those not enrolled in their courses, how they listen to the community's concerns, how they structure significant public conversations. These indicators of engagement are as worthy of note as what happens through more traditional teaching and learning.

External Resource Allocation

Best Practices

- Involve top administrators on community boards and in community initiatives.
- Encourage faculty to take leadership in the "scholarship of engagement" in their fields.
- Set aside a major portion of work-study funds for community engagement work to build a student "culture of service."

THE INDICATORS DEFINED: EXTERNAL RESOURCE ALLOCATION

- The college helps community partners create a richer learning environment for students working in the community and assists them in accessing human, technical, and intellectual resources on campus.
- The college makes resources available for community-building efforts in local neighborhoods.
- Campus mechanisms have been designed and developed to serve both the campus and the local community (e.g., shared-use buildings).
- The college has intentionally developed purchasing and hiring policies that favor local residents and businesses.

- Provide community members with access to campus facilities.
- Seek college-community grants and private-sector alliances to enhance economic development.

The Indicators in Action

Perhaps the single most important resource engaged colleges make available to their communities is their people: their administrators, their faculty, their staff, their students. As President Cowan says in her introduction to a Middlesex Community College publication entitled *The Power of Partnership:*

> Through the years, Middlesex Community College has developed many dynamic partnerships. Most of these involved the creation of unique solutions to educational dilemmas for neighboring school districts, area businesses, and organizations, as well as many foreign countries. These innovative partnerships have played a significant role in the growth of the college and the communities we serve.

Indeed, President Cowan has made effective partnerships a hallmark of her administration, and has done so beginning with an exemplary commitment of her own time and energy. Not only does she sit on dozens of community boards, she also strategically invests her time so she can be most active, in her own words, "at the beginning of new ventures and when trouble-shooting is needed." Recently she helped the local United Way go through a major reorganization. Together with her peer at Northern Essex Community College, she has entered into an agreement to provide financial support for the Merrimack Valley Economic Development Council, an important agency that lost its funding.

Perhaps the single most important resource engaged colleges make available to their communities is their people.

However, it is not just what President Cowan chooses to do that makes her such a significant community resource. She also expects and encourages her deans to show similar initiative. As she explains, "the college has a responsibility to provide resources to the community and seeks to hire people who understand the need to communicate with the community." In seeking out others with a similar sense of community commitment, she has vastly increased the college's ability to be there for the community.

For example, when one of Middlesex Community College's partners could not get the state to take seriously the need for better credentialing of local human service workers, she turned to Dean Pamela Edington for help. Eventually the dean, working with the Department of Mental Retardation, succeeded in developing and implementing a statewide certificate through the community college system. As this partner concluded, Dean Edington is "always an advocate."

President Zerrie Campbell at Malcolm X expects no less of herself and her staff. Indeed, for President Campbell, "students" may be a misleading word:

> ...the meaning of "our students" is beyond the traditional interpretation. Our community residents, the employees of our business and industry partners, the K-12 students and the parents of our service area schools are also "our students."

Given such an understanding, it is only to be expected that she would want "every one of my administrators to be on community boards," that she would try to "find the time for them to make a contribution to the community," and that she would encourage "faculty and administrators [to] work as 'teams' with 15 service area K-12 schools."

At most colleges, it is customary to ask faculty to identify their academic achievements and institutional contributions: publications, presentations, new courses, committee work, student advising. At Yakima Valley Community College, faculty have been asked to identify the ways in which they collaborate with the local community. And while much of what they have identified reflects the kind of disciplinary expertise most faculty can—and often do—make available outside the academy, some of their listings suggest far more than business as usual. For example, according to an internal document highlighting recent community outreach in the arts and sciences, "math and science faculty [have taken] leadership in a K-14 consortium to bring math and science teachers in Educational District 105 and community college faculty together to collaborate on topics of mutual concern." To date, these topics have included curricular alignment, shared best practices, shared equipment, and development of a resource inventory guide.

Community college faculty are as capable of undertaking the "scholarship of engagement" in its various forms as are their four-year colleagues.

Indeed, community college faculty are as capable of undertaking the "scholarship of engagement" in its various forms as are their four-year colleagues. At Middlesex, humanities professor Jean Trounstine has spent more than ten years teaching drama to the inmates at Framingham Women's Prison. One result of this initiative is Trounstine's recent book *Shakespeare Behind Bars: The Power of Drama in a Women's Prison* (St. Martin's, 2001), a text that deconstructs in an accessible, gripping way the image of women prisoners as "damaged goods."

John Berestecky, professor of microbiology at Kapio'lani, is deeply engaged not only in the local community but also in activities around the globe. His work has included an advisory and support role in helping numerous community-based organizations develop quality of life initiatives for people with HIV/AIDS; a leadership role in a system-wide initiative establishing Safe Zones for lesbian, gay, bisexual, and transgender students; and a mentoring role in the American Association of Community Colleges's national HIV/AIDS prevention project, "Bridges to Healthy Communities." A former Peace Corps worker in Liberia, he continues to be active in the Friends of Liberia Committee.

Just as it is not difficult to find examples of faculty who have taken their professional expertise outside the academy, so it is not difficult to find students who regularly volunteer at a variety of community sites. However, when student voluntary service goes beyond random individual interest, we can begin to speak of a student culture of service.

One of the best examples we found of the latter is at Yakima Valley, where the student body as a whole can be seen as a powerful community resource. Nine hundred students per year (out of an enrollment of just over 4,000) tutor at 43 sites around the Yakima Valley—at hospitals, childcare centers, and doctors' offices, as well as in schools—and are trained both on and off campus for their work. Forty percent of the college's work-study budget is set aside for its engaged students, and many student club activities have a community connection. Meanwhile, the administration supports broad collaborations around early childhood education, and local businesses provide rewards for children who become eager readers.

Workforce development programs can also be seen as a community resource in that they improve the community's chances of attracting and retaining private-sector investments.

A college's employees and students may be its most valuable community resource, but they are clearly not its only resource. At several schools we also found an extraordinary willingness to share campus facilities with off-campus groups. At Middlesex, a dean stated that the community has "an open invitation to use [the college's] facilities and programs," and, therefore, "the facilities people are very important resources." The same dean explained:

> When the Lowell campus opened, the idea behind it was that the community should use the campus in the same way it used local school space—whenever there were legitimate needs that didn't conflict with scheduled teaching/learning activities. Over 800 people a year attend different kinds of support groups on campus. There is a sense that "this place belongs to you." Even city hall makes use of the campus's resources.

At Malcolm X, the story is similar. Seeing itself as "the social and cultural hub of West Chicago," the college willingly shares its space with the surrounding community. The largest Kwanzaa celebration in the country is held on campus. The college sponsors career fairs for the Chicago public schools. Elementary schools use the campus for their graduation ceremonies. Even the mayor holds events there. According to President Campbell, "Over 100,000 participants enjoyed the educational and cultural facilities at Malcolm X College during the more than 900 events sponsored/hosted during the last fiscal year."

Finally, there is money. Although we found no community college able to make cash donations to the community, we found several whose skill in pursuing college-community grants has resulted in an important infusion of local aid. For example, Middlesex Community College has provided matching funds for faculty who have won outside grants to work in the prisons, and Yakima Valley is a partner in an $11 million Gear Up grant with local schools in eight different districts. These colleges have been so successful in this regard that it is difficult to imagine what their communities would look like without them.

Economic development assistance can take many forms: a presidential task force, creative partnering with local businesses, institutional investment in underserved neighborhoods. But workforce development programs—long a primary community college responsibility—can also be seen as a community resource in that they improve the community's chances of attracting and retaining private-sector investments.

However, developing private-sector partnerships may require different skills than does working with the nonprofit sector. Middlesex is one school that has had a great deal of success in seeking out and fostering partnerships with local and national businesses. The college's Office of Institutional Research seeks the input of area businesses and convenes groups around their interests. Then the Office of Business and Industry follows these initiatives with concrete plans and activities to meet identified needs. Anne Arundel Community College has had similar success, and in 2001 the college received the National Alliance of Business (NAB) Community College of the Year Distinguished Performance Award. The award recognized a number of the college's innovative practices, including contract training initiatives developed in cooperation with companies such as Northrop Grumman.

EXAMPLE FROM THE FIELD: ANNUAL REPORT TO THE COMMUNITY

As the President of Malcolm X College, I am proud to say that we are committed to student success. Our mission, "Empowerment through Education," reflects our pledge to provide students with the most relevant curricula paired with the most innovative teaching and learning methods to assist them in attaining their educational goals. In addition to our commitment to academic excellence, we are committed to extending student learning experiences beyond the classroom setting to the global community through cultural programs and extracurricular activities.

This report tells you that the meaning of "our students" is beyond the traditional interpretation. Our community residents, the employees of our business and industry partners, the K-12 students and the parents of our service area schools are also "our students." As a community college, we serve the community when we build a community of learners.

I welcome you to visit our college to talk with our students, faculty and staff. I am sure their personal narration and reflection will be more convincing than this report.

Thank you for taking your time to review this report to the community. To learn more about Malcolm X College, its programs, services and activities, please visit our website at Malcolmx.ccc.edu or call....

Warmest Regards,

Zerrie D. Campbell
President

—From Malcolm X Community College, introduction to Annual Report to the Community, 2002

Community Voice

Best Practices

- Establish communication vehicles such as focus groups, community meetings, newsletters, and reports to the community.
- Give community members a say in setting college priorities.
- Customize college activities—both outreach and academic—to meet local needs.

The Indicators in Action

It is ironic, but the ability and willingness to play the kind of community role colleges like Yakima Valley, Malcolm X, and Middlesex have played marks them as anything but power brokers. Granted, as President Cowan has said, Middlesex as a whole does try "to function as an 'honest broker.'" However, this role implies not an ability to call the shots but an ability to "[leverage] resources (including new revenue streams) that

THE INDICATORS DEFINED: COMMUNITY VOICE

- Community partners are deeply and regularly involved in determining their role in and contribution to community-based learning.
- Community partners play a significant role in helping shape institutional involvement in the community.
- Community partners are well represented on all relevant college-based committees.
- Community partners provide feedback on the development and maintenance of engagement programs and are involved in all relevant strategic planning.
- The college allocates resources to compensate community partners for their participation in service-learning courses.

can benefit the community." Indeed, if anything characterizes institutions like these, it is the ability to listen.

Civic and community engagement, we found, cannot simply be equated with successful outreach. True engagement assumes a fundamental shift in the way a college regards the community in which it is embedded. In this model, the college does not act unilaterally on matters affecting the community, however benign its intentions. Instead, it recognizes the community as its complementary equal, fully entitled to speak out on and to participate in all matters of common concern. What an accreditation committee recently said of Anne Arundel—"You are the community's college"—applies equally to many other colleges.

A willingness to listen carefully to the community takes many forms. At Yakima Valley, for example, President Linda Kaminski held a series of "For a Better Tomorrow" community meetings for the community to help the college set its present course. The college also organizes community focus groups before any new program starts. Its quarterly *Campus Update* goes to every household in the community.

At Anne Arundel, the college not only operates 120 local sites where it offers some kind of learning, it also solicits a "wish list" from its community partners, and has begun organizing on-campus forums where agencies speak to faculty and staff about some issue central to the agencies' work. Perhaps the most impressive example of the college's commitment to maintaining communication with its non-campus constituents is its "Report to the Community," an attractive and easily readable booklet that walks constituents through the college's recent accomplishments, exemplary programs and partnerships, and enrollment and budget profiles. The publication even includes photos of individuals from the community as well as from the college.

At Portland Community College, Neal Naigus's position as Community Relations Manager obviously focuses directly and emphatically on the community and its issues. As Naigus explains: "I organize numerous public forums that engage both the students and the community. My job is unique; it is focused on service to the community." He also emphasizes that community members as well as campus groups can suggest issues of public interest around which they want to convene.

Like most community colleges, all these schools make ample use of community advisory boards with regard to their pre-professional programs. But in some cases, especially where the need is great, this campus-community connection becomes anything but casual. The role that a college like Malcolm X plays in producing health care professionals for the community cannot be overestimated. Further, the training it provides is often customized to meet specific needs identified by local institutions and practitioners.

Customized is the key word here. For unlike many college-community relationships where the college initiates or maintains a program in good faith and in accordance with generally accepted practice, calling upon the community only to ratify its choices and perhaps to suggest minor adjustments, what we found again and again among these colleges is a willingness to follow the community's priorities. At Yakima Valley, for example, if the community identifies a pressing need for more English as a second language (ESL) instruction, the college mobilizes in response. When Malcolm X discovers a major drop-off in students' writing and grammar skills owing to a cutback in grammar instruction in the public schools, it responds with a new emphasis on grammar and writing instruction. Whether the issue is asthma, childcare, paraprofessional training, or aging, these colleges can be counted on to hear—and to respond.

Whether the issue is asthma, childcare, para-professional training, or aging, these colleges can be counted on to hear—and to respond.

Forums for Fostering Public Dialogue

Best Practices

- Convene campus and community members to discuss local and national issues of mutual relevance.
- Provide training for students and faculty in moderating public dialogue.
- Coordinate the work of external affairs, student affairs, and other offices to create broad initiatives that involve multiple constituencies.
- Involve legislators and other public officials in dialogues to give community members a channel to government decision-makers.

THE INDICATORS DEFINED:
FORUMS FOR FOSTERING PUBLIC DIALOGUE

- The college plays a visible and effective role in facilitating dialogue around important public issues.
- The college helps to bring together stakeholders from all sectors of the community.

The Indicators in Action

Our final indicator of civic engagement turns on a college's willingness to serve as the community's convener in discussing public issues. In this regard, many of the colleges we looked at play exemplary roles.

As has already been mentioned, Neal Naigus's position as Portland's Community Relations Manager has as one of its major responsibilities a convening function. As someone who has been active in the "Deliberative Democracy" project of the Kettering Foundation and has served as the director of the Pacific Northwest Public

Policy Institute for eight years, Naigus has trained dozens of students and faculty to moderate public deliberations. Portland has sponsored forums on planned parenthood, local ballot measures, diversity, and national issues like military intervention and anti-war activities.

At Middlesex, the Student Life Office sponsors a "One World Series" for both students and the wider community. The series has addressed topics such as steroid abuse, sexual harassment, attention deficit disorder, human rights violations, AIDS, breast cancer, and violence in society. In addition, the president's office, the campus manager, and the Office of External Affairs all serve as vehicles of convening. Indeed, one of the most impressive aspects of the college's work as a community convener is the multi-dimensionality of its efforts. While on one level it is sponsoring its One World Series and its even more prestigious Celebrity Series, on another level it runs a City Symposium with various individual partners, and on still another level it convenes special luncheons for eighth-grade girls.

EXAMPLE FROM THE FIELD: CONNECTING CAMPUS TO COMMUNITY THROUGH PUBLIC DIALOGUE

"With the One World series, we want to challenge students to think about issues that society as a whole deals with—to 'tune in' more," explained Dennis Malvers, Associate Dean of Student Development, who plans the speaker series through MCC's Student Life Office. "We also hope to challenge students to think about these issues a little bit differently than they might have in the past."

Malvers also works closely with the surrounding community to book speakers that might be of interest to local residents. "Our target audience with One World is the public, as well as the campus community," he explains. "We have great participation from Bedford High School students and community leaders. And we've collaborated with the Lowell and Bedford school systems in booking speakers," said Malvers. "We welcome input from outside agencies and community groups."

—Excerpted from Middlesex Community College, "The One World Series: Bringing the Outside World—with All Its Difference—to Campus," Profiles of People, Programs, and Partnerships, *Spring 2001, p.5.*

At Malcolm X, where there is a similar breath of venues, issues, and participants, an especially interesting initiative is the series of "town hall" meetings hosted by Congressman Danny K. Davis. Through this series, the community not only finds a public voice; it also finds a way to take its concerns directly to its Washington representative. As a vehicle of civic engagement, the college's town hall meetings help restore some sense of having a reliable channel between the local and the federal.

Depending on the make-up of each college's communities, forums like the ones discussed here can either give underserved populations an all too rare opportunity to experience the kind of public deliberation on which functional democracy is based, or give majority populations an opportunity to hear and to take into account positions they seldom consider. In both cases, the college plays a role not dissimilar to the one played by small town meetings where unpopular as well as popular positions are put on the table, where those with means must share the spotlight with those whose needs are poorly met. In this way the community college as convener naturally complements the community college as sponsor of community-based teaching and learning.

Conclusion: Community Colleges and the Promise of a Diverse Democracy

> *"Democracy needs to be reborn in every generation, and education is its midwife."*
>
> JOHN DEWEY (1916)

Community Colleges and Democratic Infrastructure

As the results of the research reported here suggest, community colleges are positioned to become not just a component but a central building block in America's democratic infrastructure. By implementing service-learning and civic engagement strategies, they are demonstrably improving the quality of life in the communities they serve while at the same time enhancing learning outcomes for an increasingly diverse student population. They are frontline institutions in the struggle to create a truly inclusive twenty-first century democracy.

They are, moreover, indispensable in contemporary efforts to reconnect the academy to a tradition of education for the common good. As William Sullivan (1999) writes in an essay entitled "The University as Citizen: Institutional Identity and Social Responsibility,"

> In the absence of an updated version of its founding conception of itself as a participant in the life of civil society, as a citizen of American democracy, much of higher education has come to operate on a sort of default program of instrumental individualism. This is the familiar notion that the academy exists to research and disseminate knowledge and skills as tools for economic development and the upward mobility of individuals. This "default program" of instrumental individualism leaves the larger questions of social, political, and moral purpose out of explicit consideration (p. 21).

Just how far the community colleges profiled here are from this "default program" a glance at our chapter on institutional culture will quickly make apparent. There one finds mission statements, strategic plans, and administrative/academic leaders that in no sense shy away from "explicit consideration" of their institutions' public purposes. This sense of public commitment was confirmed over and over again by the community partners with whom we spoke—mostly in sessions at which no college personnel were present. Surely such colleges offer a lesson not only to their peer institutions but to American higher education in general on how one maintains trust with a democratic tradition.

But the lesson they offer is not just for higher education. In state after state it is often the community colleges that feel most severely the effects of budget cutbacks. For example, from 2001 to 2003, Virginia cut $55 million in state funds from the budget for its community colleges (Morse, 2003). In California, the state's fiscal crisis is forcing deep cuts in education. Despite Proposition 98, a state law mandating that community colleges receive 10.9% of the money set aside for K-14 education, in 2003-2004 the state's community colleges received only 9.6% of available funds (Hebel, 2003). Relatedly, when major foundations look for models and pilot programs to fund, they most often look to four-year schools—often those very schools whose endowments afford them considerable fiscal security. Thus, instead of investing in that educational sector where both the need and the potential for public engagement are greatest, public and private resources are channeled away from where they could, arguably, do the most good.

The community colleges profiled here offer a lesson not only to their peer institutions but to American higher education in general on how one maintains trust with a democratic tradition.

Take, for example, the role of community colleges in educating underprepared students. Unlike the education of "upwardly mobile individuals" (Sullivan, 1999, p. 21), the education of students from underserved communities is an issue that affects far more than the individuals directly involved. Indeed, according to Alexander Astin and colleagues (2000), "if we fail to develop more effective means for educating 'remedial students,' we will find it difficult to make much headway in resolving some of our most pressing social and economic problems" (p. 130). For this reason, they regard the education of such students as "the most important educational problem in America today."

But according to the demographer Samuel Kipp (in Gladieux and Swail, 1998, p. 112), trends suggest change in precisely the opposite direction: as we approach 2010, the college-age population will be increasingly less well prepared for educational success.

> While the pool of high school graduates and college students will increase substantially...the most rapid growth will occur among groups traditionally more likely to drop out of school, less likely to enroll in college-preparatory course work, less likely to graduate from high school, less likely to enroll in college, and least likely to persist to earn a baccalaureate degree.

Hence, Gladieux and Swail conclude:

> If demography is destiny, colleges have their work cut out for them....America is still an ongoing experiment in diversity, and higher education's part of the social contract has been to extend the possibility of a better life to new groups in society. It will be in the enlightened self-interest of institutions to invest more heavily in partnerships with school systems to expand the potential college-bound and qualified pool. Reaching out to help motivate and prepare more students for college is a long-term investment that will pay off for higher education and the nation (p. 112).

For community colleges to meet the challenge of underprepared students—for a large percentage of them will inevitably show up on their doorsteps—those colleges will need not only increased funding but also a new level of recognition and respect as befits their critical civic role. Such recognition and respect must include a clear understanding of the distinctive forms civic engagement and service-learning take in the community college context.

For community colleges to meet the challenge of underprepared students, they will need not only increased funding but also a new level of recognition and respect as befits their critical civic role.

A Distinctive Profile

As noted in the introduction to this volume, the primary goal of the research reported here is to identify some specific ways in which Campus Compact's "indicators of engagement" are put into effect at community colleges. On the basis of our findings, we offer the following observations as a conceptual framework within which civic engagement and service-learning at community colleges can best be understood and appreciated:

1. The community college can itself be viewed as a community-based organization: It is *of*, not simply *in*, a particular place.

2. Community-based course assignments complement a mission in which "to reach" and "to teach" are two facets of a single responsibility.

3. The culture of a community college, especially as modeled by its president and her/his administration—together with hiring practices that stress participation in that culture—plays a critical role in generating and sustaining faculty interest in community-based work.

4. The primacy of teaching and learning as institutional priorities helps elevate pedagogical effectiveness above purely disciplinary concerns.

5. Civic engagement strategies often relate to and help deliver workforce-readiness skills.

6. Both student demographics and faculty teaching load affect the kinds of community-based assignments offered in service-learning courses.

7. The relative absence of "mission creep" and the relative unimportance of research university norms allow for a more flexible understanding of faculty roles and rewards.

8. Effective "enabling mechanisms"—and a willingness to fund them even in difficult economic circumstances—are in most cases essential to the success of service-learning as an institutional strategy.

9. One especially important way in which the college assists the community is by acting as a broker and an active listener. As a result, relationships are truly reciprocal.

These observations, in turn, can be bundled into three general points. First, civically engaged community colleges see themselves as actual members of their communities to a far greater extent than is true for most liberal arts colleges and most universities. Hence, insofar as a renewal of civic commitment is emerging as a hallmark of the contemporary academy, community colleges have a unique opportunity to explore what Ernest Boyer (1996a, p. 20) calls a "special climate in which the academic and the civic cultures communicate more continuously and creatively with each other." And in doing so they can make a significant contribution to the academy as a whole.

Second, several observations point to the possibility of an *institutional* commitment to civic engagement that is sufficiently strong and comprehensive to inform how the institution works in all its constituent parts. Whereas the mode of operation of the research university—in which disciplinary identity and individual achievement trump all other considerations—frequently makes itself felt even at other kinds of four-year institutions, this is not the case at engaged community colleges. Shared vision and collective action are by no means impossible. Given effective administrative leadership, the relative absence of a disciplinary "guild" culture leaves room for a civic effort that can be owned by every college constituency, if not every individual constituency member.

Shared vision and collective action are by no means impossible.

Third, the actual practice of service-learning follows a path somewhat different from that followed at most four-year schools. Community-based assignments can deliver valued skills and insights not closely linked to a unique course content. Student engagement and motivation "count" as valid assignment outcomes. Civic, pre-professional, and academic considerations blur. Making possible the very existence of this fluid field of engagement is an infrastructure that provides not only logistical assistance but also a placement process that further distances community-based work from a narrower understanding of course relevance. In short, what is seen as academically valid service-learning includes more than would be possible at other kinds of institutions.

Service-Learning and the Needs of a Diverse Student Body

That the identity, culture, and pedagogical profile of community colleges lend themselves so well to community-based work is fortunate for several reasons. In an article entitled "New Students—New Learning Styles" (*Change,* Sept./Oct. 1993, p. 22), Charles Schroeder discusses a study that found that

> approximately 60 percent of entering students prefer [a] sensing mode of perceiving [compared with] 40 percent who prefer [an] intuitive mode. The learning styles of those who prefer sensing are characterized by a preference for direct, concrete experiences; moderate to high degrees of structure; linear, sequential learning; and, often, a need to know why before doing something. In general, students who prefer sensing learning patterns prefer the concrete, the practical, and the immediate.

While it is clearly important to recognize that not all community college students fall into the "sensing" category, Schroeder notes that many community college students do "lack confidence in their intellectual abilities and are uncomfortable with abstract ideas" (p. 24). Thus, if Schroeder is correct, and "the path to educational excellence" for such students is "a practice-to-theory route, not the more traditional theory-to-practice approach" (p. 24), teaching/learning strategies like service-learning acquire even greater institutional importance. While more intellectually confident and competent students can use their community-based experiences to develop higher order thinking skills (Marchese, 1996), less advanced students can develop through those same experiences both personal motivation and a concrete sense of achievement.

The fact that community-based work can address the needs of both more and less developed learners makes it invaluable as part of an institutional "bridge" strategy. As Bailey (2003, p. 4) notes, closing the opportunity gap and raising the bar of achievement will require "finding and exploiting complementarities" in community colleges' multiple missions. By connecting academic study with meaningful service in the community, service-learning represents just such a complementarity. While service-learning helps students of various kinds develop academically, it also exposes them to experiences that can better inform their choice of majors or careers. While acquiring intellectual skills valued by their professors, they simultaneously learn skills and work habits highly valued by potential employers. Thus, the multiple responsibilities of the community college—preparation for work, for citizenship, and for academic transfer—can be addressed in a naturally balanced, interconnected manner.

Recommendations

While it is of paramount importance that we recognize and make room for the distinctive forms civic engagement and service-learning take at community colleges, it is also important to recognize some of the distinctive challenges community colleges face in attempting to improve their practice. Thus, for example, our research suggests that community colleges would be well served if their understanding of service-learning, its rationale, and its uses were even more carefully articulated and monitored. Precisely because community colleges are engaged with their communities in so many different ways and on so many different levels, it is relatively easy for them to let one form of engagement slide into another. When this happens with service-learning, and service-learning is allowed to slide into either community service or traditional pre-professional field work, its distinctive academic and civic benefits can be compromised. While the greater flexibility most community colleges allow for service-learning practice represents a strength, that strength can turn into a liability if extended too far. Academic "quality control" is a must if the community college contribution to civic renewal is to be widely recognized and supported.

Academic "quality control" is a must if the community college contribution to civic renewal is to be widely recognized and supported.

Another area that deserves special attention is academic-community collaboration. While college-community collaboration in general represents an obvious community college strength, we found that more consultation might be desirable in some areas. For example, many community colleges convene practitioner advisory groups to help with the design and implementation of pre-professional programs. However, we found little to suggest that community partners are similarly involved in the design of service-learning assignments. Their *academic* role seems to be limited to helping to facilitate reflection. Similarly, the community is less well represented on relevant college committees and in relevant strategic planning processes than we might have predicted. Nor do many colleges seem to have the resources to compensate community partners for their assistance, whatever its extent, aside from recognition luncheons and the like.

Given the extent to which the colleges featured in this volume do collaborate with the community, pointing out such omissions may seem ungenerous. Nevertheless, insofar as community colleges really do set the bar for substantive college-community partnering, it is important we keep in mind the full spectrum of possible arrangements—even if at present some seem rather utopian.

Not at all utopian is the issue of adjuncts and their role in achieving an engaged campus. Since approximately two-thirds of community college faculty are adjuncts (Phillippe and Patton, 2000), many of whom teach the introductory core courses in English and math, any comprehensive engagement strategy must take the special needs of this group into account. Books such as *The Invisible Faculty* (Gappa and Leslie, 1993) and *Ghosts in the Classroom* (Dubson, 2001) describe the adjunct experience as undefined and inequitable. Indeed, the use of "invisible" and "ghosts" in these titles suggests that many adjuncts enjoy little visibility within their own college communities. Furthermore, adjuncts themselves are a varied group. They may be people with careers who have taught courses for decades, individuals who want to work only a limited number of hours each week, or faculty who teach part-time at multiple institutions in hopes of securing a full-time position. While this diversity can provide many opportunities for community engagement—at the same time helping adjuncts define themselves within the college in more visible ways—such opportunities need to be deliberately cultivated.

Adjuncts who also work at community agencies can quickly become true pioneers in establishing important academic-community collaborations.

Since many adjuncts do not have offices or phones on campus, establishing a reliable connection with them is a critical first step. Then, providing a large menu of options for them to obtain more information about service-learning and civic engagement—e.g., online orientations, departmental mentors, and college workshops—can help accommodate their varying needs. Many will welcome an invitation to participate in service-learning projects and may well serve as resources for new service sites as well as insights about emerging local issues.

Indeed, adjuncts who also work at community agencies can quickly become true pioneers in establishing important academic-community collaborations and in creating partnership models for others to consider. The dual identity of these faculty members/community partners can help them emerge as cultural brokers, translating between the academic lexicon and community realities. Their understanding of the nuances of each culture can be invaluable in keeping implementation problems to a minimum and in leading to more successful collaboration strategies. For example, a local principal who teaches a course on urban schools can engage her college students in addressing real K-12 problems while at the same time strengthening their commitment to civic responsibility. Rather than remaining invisible, adjuncts can learn to play a central role in defining a campus that is truly engaged with its surrounding community.

Campus Compact's Ongoing Commitment to Community Colleges

The mission of Campus Compact is to support the civic goals of higher education. As the profiles included in this volume suggest, for many community colleges, institutional mission and civic mission are largely one and the same. In this regard, these schools provide a model of how all institutions of higher education can better fulfill their civic purposes. Furthermore, as we have noted, the work of community colleges all too often goes unrecognized and underappreciated both by policymakers and by administrators and faculty at four-year institutions. It is our hope that publication of this monograph will help to dispel the relative ignorance that exists regarding the civic impact and the civic achievement of community colleges, and that more four-year faculty and administrators will begin to learn from their two-year peers.

NEW RESOURCE FOR COMMUNITY COLLEGES

Campus Compact recently launched a new website for community colleges that includes resources to support civic and community engagement, updates on the Indicators of Engage-ment Project, grant opportunities, upcoming events, and more. See www.compact.org/community-colleges.

Ideally, Campus Compact's Indicators of Engagement Project will both help support community colleges in their continued efforts to engage with their communities and bring increased attention to the cutting-edge work already taking place at many community colleges across the country. It is our hope that community colleges will see this book not only as a useful publication vis-à-vis civic and community engagement but also as a pledge of Campus Compact's ongoing commitment to work with them in fulfilling the promise of a diverse democracy.

Appendix I: Research Methodology

Evaluation Framework

The 13 indicators of engagement represent characteristics that align college/university resources with the needs of various communities to address social, civic, economic, and moral problems (Boyer, 1996b; Hollander, Saltmarsh, and Zlotkowski, 2001). The project team devised a detailed evaluation process to determine which characteristics promote institutional effectiveness by bringing together civic education and local community concerns. Because no one campus manifested all 13 indicators of engagement, the project team chose to evaluate each indicator separately rather than to focus on the colleges with the most indicators. This approach allowed greater insight into how the indicators are put into practice and into the extent to which the indicators reflect institutional engagement.

The evaluation design was derived from the primary goal of the project: *To identify, document, and disseminate best practices of civic engagement that demonstrated successful strategies for each of the 13 indicators of engagement, using exemplars from community colleges.* The focus was on evaluating short-term impacts that were measurable within the one-year time frame of the community college phase of the project. While the overall project goal sought to highlight successful strategies of exemplary practice, an important component of the evaluation design was to identify lessons learned and opportunities for improvement related to the indicators of engagement, as well as to cite areas of accomplishment. In this way, learning from the first year's work with community colleges could inform the subsequent years of the Compact's overall Indicators of Engagement Project.

Evaluation of higher education programs, especially those that focus on community engagement, must be practical and defined within a reasonable scope (Gelmon, Holland, et al., 2001). Thus the evaluation design for this project involved a process common to both community-based and higher education programs. That process included the following steps to create an evaluation matrix (Figure 1).

- Define key concepts for the evaluation that reflect the program and evaluation goals (what do we want to know?).
- Determine specific measurable or observable indicators or identifiers for each concept (how will we know it through measurable or observable descriptors?).
- Develop unique instruments or adapt existing ones appropriate to the indicator (what methods will we use to collect this evidence?).

FIGURE 1: EVALUATION MATRIX

Key Concepts *What do we want to know?*	**Key Indicators** *How will we know it?*	**Methods/Sources** *What methods will we use to collect the evidence?*
Identification of exemplary practices of service-learning and civic engagement	Documented evidence of: – Innovation – Sustainability – Replicability – Significance – Intentionality – Recognition – Institutionalization – Transformative effect	Web-based screening survey Telephone follow-up screening survey Site visit protocol Supplemental site visitor survey Documentation review Supplemental information collection
Refinement of indicators of engagement	Operationalized indicators Testing of indicators in different markets and geographic contexts Revisions to clarify indicators	Panel review Surveys Site visits
Dissemination of findings	Awareness among community colleges Knowledge of policymakers Sharing of best practices Use and application in multiple institutions	Presentations Publications Web resources Policy advocacy State Compact use

Methods of Evaluation

The process of assessing campus programs included an extensive internal evaluation process to define project tasks, scope, and timelines; develop and refine protocols and procedures; and "operationalize" the indicators of engagement to translate them from their initial conceptual form into more specific measurable and/or observable language. Through ongoing collaboration, project leaders and the evaluation team integrated the evaluation perspective into program planning and delivery from the outset, ensuring that the evaluation team had a detailed understanding of project elements at all stages, and that the project team was always aware of opportunities for program improvement or modifications in project strategy through continuous evaluation.

Operationalizing the Indicators of Engagement

Initial working sessions with Campus Compact staff and with Campus Compact's Community College Engaged Scholars provided the groundwork to operationalize language for each of the 13 indicators of engagement. This process involved posing key questions to elicit both evidence of the indicators' presence and a context for how the indicators are demonstrated on community college campuses. This work helped to articulate the concepts underlying each indicator and the specific meanings of the language in the indicators' descriptors (described in the Introduction). This process also included developing a list of documents and other evidence that could be reviewed and would illustrate the variety of ways the indicators might be made evident on campuses.

The team also articulated terms defining the phrase "exemplary practice." These definitional aids were developed to ensure a common understanding among all project staff regarding exemplary practices of civic engagement and to standardize measurement and observation of particular indicators. The language developed to define what is meant by "exemplary" included the following eight characteristics:

- Innovative: new, special, groundbreaking
- Sustainable: continued, results used
- Replicable: transferable elsewhere
- Significant: makes a difference in mission
- Intentional: deliberate, planned, systematic
- Recognized: acknowledged, understood
- Institutionalized: integrated, part of culture
- Transforming: improves life, moves to goals

To observe and test the key indicators or identifiers of each concept included in Figure 1, the project staff and evaluators designed a mix of quantitative and qualitative methods. These methods included a range of data collection strategies, including surveys, interviews, focus groups, reflection activities, observations, documentation review, and data analysis. The overall evaluation design built upon existing reliable and validated instruments, to the extent these were available. New instruments were designed when necessary and tailored to meet the specific needs of the project. The following paragraphs describe the design and development of each method.

Campus Compact Survey of Exemplary Practices

In order to gather information from community colleges on their approaches to civic engagement, project staff needed access to community colleges. While community colleges make up more than 20% of the Compact's membership, project staff were committed to including the broadest possible range of institutions in this study. In order to reach community colleges that are not Compact members, project staff collaborated with the American Association of Community Colleges (AACC), whose membership includes almost 95% of all two-year colleges in the United States.

IOEP staff, working with their partners at the AACC, created a web-based survey to seek self-reporting by community colleges on the presence of exemplary practices or approaches as defined by the indicators of engagement. The survey asked for minimal descriptive information about the community college and then offered the opportunity to describe exemplary practices or approaches for as many of the indicators as the campus chose to report. Campus Compact and the AACC publicized the survey through email announcements (including an announcement to all 1,100 AACC members), postings on the organizations' websites, personal contacts, and conference announcements. The announcements included a request that the individual with the broadest knowledge of the college's work in civic engagement respond to the survey. The survey was accessed through the AACC website. Twenty-four institutions completed the survey; 19 of these, or 79%, were Compact members.

Initial Telephone Screening Interview Protocol

To gain further understanding of the survey responses, the evaluation team developed a telephone interview protocol for project staff to elicit additional information from the most promising survey responses. The interview protocol contained five questions related to the indicators of engagement designed to aid project staff in selecting colleges that would receive site visits. These open-ended questions were intended to elicit a diverse and more comprehensive range of responses than was feasible in the initial survey. The protocol also allowed interviewers to seek clarification of responses to the Compact survey and to probe to determine whether the self-identified practices were truly "exemplary." The five questions, which were identical for each self-identified indicator, are as follows:

1. *"Explain how this practice might be unique compared to other approaches you have tried before or to similar practices of which you may be aware. In other words, how is this practice especially significant?"*

2. *"Please give me concrete examples of what makes this indicator exemplary."*

3. *"Was there a deliberate or intentional effort to implement this practice? I'd like to hear more about the details of how the approach was established on your campus."*

4. *"I'd also like you to tell me how well this approach has been accepted on campus. Is there widespread support for the practice among your colleagues and the administration [or students and the community, if applicable to this indicator]?"*

5. *"Finally, I'd like you to explain how this practice might be a transforming mechanism in terms of helping to institutionalize service-learning and civic engagement on your campus."*

The two Engaged Scholars and two members of the project staff conducted telephone interviews with 20 of the survey respondents. The results of the interviews were used in the selection of sites to be visited, described in the next section.

Selection of Colleges to Receive Site Visits

The project team selected sites to visit on the basis of several pre-defined parameters. To ensure the broadest applicability of results, it was important to promote campus diversity across the sites. Among the factors the project team considered in selecting the schools were geographic region, campus size, and the demographic context (i.e., urban or rural setting). A primary concern was to ensure consistency in the number of indicators assessed both at each site visit and across visits; therefore, the team determined that each indicator would be assessed during at least two site visits, and that no site visit would address more than three indicators.

Following each telephone interview, the interviewer identified three to four potentially exemplary indicators for that campus. A decision matrix developed by the evaluation team aided in the selection process. The matrix matched the prospective sites by indicator and accounted for the demographic and other factors (see Figure 2). As a result of this evaluation, the project team selected 13 sites to receive visits, representing a diversity of community colleges based on geography, size, and other descriptive factors. In some cases, sites offered more than three potentially exemplary indicators, but only three were selected to ensure that site visits would be manageable.

Selection of Schools to Be Profiled

Among the colleges that responded to the survey, several that were not chosen to receive site visits offered a particularly innovative program or approach to engagement. Project staff felt these colleges deserved further recognition because they had valuable information to share with community colleges and the rest of field. As a result, project staff decided to profile programs from these institutions, based on the telephone interviews and follow-up conversations, in this monograph. These profiles, which focus on a particularly significant program or characteristic related to one of the indicators of engagement, add to the perspectives on the indicators. Figure 3 lists the additional institutions profiled in this monograph.

FIGURE 2: COLLEGES AND INDICATORS SELECTED FOR SITE VISITS

College Name	Rural/ Urban	Size	INDICATORS												
			1	2	3	4	5	6	7	8	9	10	11	12	13
West															
Albuquerque TVI (NM)	Urban	18,800			x				x	x					
Chandler-Gilbert (AZ)	Urban	6,760		x					x				x		
Kapi'olani (HI)	Urban	7,169		x				x					x		
Portland (OR)	Urban/ Suburban	24,882	x				x							x	
Yakima Valley (WA)	Rural	2,531									x	x			x
Central															
Kirtland (MI)	Rural	1,409		x	x		x								
Malcolm X (IL)	Urban	3,169	x					x			x				
Northeast															
Middlesex (MA)	Urban	7,568	x									x		x	
Raritan Valley (NJ)	Suburban	5,830			x	x				x					
Southern Maine (ME)	Urban	2,500					x						x		x
South															
Anne Arundel (MD)	Suburban	12,815					x			x	x				
Brevard (FL)	Urban	13,681					x	x	x						
Miami Dade (FL)	Urban	53,486		x		x				x					

Indicator Code:

1. Mission and Purpose
2. Administrative and Academic Leadership
3. Disciplines, Departments, and Interdisciplinary Work
4. Pedagogy and Epistemology
5. Faculty Development
6. Faculty Roles and Rewards
7. Enabling Mechanisms
8. Internal Resource Allocation
9. Community Voice
10. External Resource Allocation
11. Integrated and Complementary Engagement Activities
12. Forums for Fostering Public Dialogue
13. Student Voice

Site Visit Interview Protocol

The next step was to develop a comprehensive interview protocol for each of the 13 indicators of engagement that could be used in a standardized manner by the three site visitors (the two Community College Engaged Scholars and the Campus

FIGURE 3: COLLEGES PROFILED

College Name	Setting	Size	Profile Indicator
College of Lake County (IL)	Suburban	14,385	Community voice
Collin County Community College District (TX)	Urban	14,497	Faculty roles and rewards
Hocking College (OH)	Rural	5,316	Disciplines and departments
Johnson County Community College (KS)	Suburban	17,776	Disciplines and departments
Mount Wachusett Community College (MA)	Rural	3,711	Community voice and enabling mechanisms
Virginia Highlands Community College (VA)	Rural	2,383	Student voice

Compact Senior Faculty Fellow). The evaluation team wrote a set of indicator-specific questions for each of four key stakeholder groups—college leaders and administrators, faculty members, students, and community partners. Some intentional redundancy was built into the protocol to ensure that key topics would be addressed across a number of indicators. Given that each visit explicitly examined only three indicators, this redundancy ensured that the site visitors addressed the key questions at each site visit.

In order to test the protocol, each of the three site visitors provided feedback on both the content and application of the site visit protocol after their first site visit. Based on the feedback, the protocol was revised to reduce the length of time necessary to conduct the interviews and to minimize redundancy within question sets.

Site Visit Supplementary Survey

Project staff were also interested in obtaining an overall assessment from the site visitors that would reflect their perceptions of each campus they visited. The evaluators thus developed a supplementary survey to assist the site visitors in judging the degree to which an indicator was exemplary. Using the descriptors developed to define "exemplary practice," the supplemental survey used a Likert–scale-type format to rate eight descriptors. At the end of each visit, the site visitor completed the survey for each of the three indicators selected for the campus and returned it to the evaluators. This supplemental survey was used as part of the overall comparative analysis of indicators examined at the selected sites.

Finally, each site visitor also wrote a brief one-page reflective narrative to record general impressions about a campus, especially as they pertained to campus-community linkages. The narrative gave the site visitors an opportunity to reflect on and integrate their findings for each campus. It also served as one more perspective to consider when determining consistency across all the data gathered on exemplary practices at the selected campuses.

Synthesis and Reporting of Site Visit Findings

The evaluation team used the descriptions for each indicator of engagement, developed by Hollander, Saltmarsh, and Zlotkowski (2001), as the framework to capture the various aspects of each exemplary practice. This involved synthesizing the site visit reports/interview transcripts, the narrative reflections, and the supplemental surveys of best practices submitted by the site visitors. For example, under the indicator *mission and purpose,* the team articulated four key features as indicative of a school's commitment to civic engagement as reflected in its mission and purpose:

- The college's mission explicitly articulates its commitment to the public purposes of higher education and higher education's civic responsibility to educate for democratic participation.
- This aspect of the mission is openly valued and is explicitly used to promote and explain the civic activities of the campus.
- The college demonstrates a genuine willingness to review, discuss, and strengthen the civic aspect of its mission.
- All campus constituencies demonstrate their familiarity with and ownership of the college's mission.

Using these descriptions as the basis for synthesis, the evaluation team focused on areas of best practice that converged or were unique among the schools visited for each indicator under review. This approach offered substantial insights into how each school interpreted and expressed its civic commitment, especially when the demographic profile of each campus was considered. The descriptions helped to show the context for engagement, which included whether and to what extent a practice had become entrenched at a school, the degree of dissemination of the engaged practices within the school and the community at large, and support for the principles of engagement among all (or some) stakeholder groups, leading to a sense of ownership of the best practices. The synthesis provided a narrative snapshot of the community college context for engagement through the demonstration of a diverse array of best practices. A similar format was used for each indicator.

Methodological Concerns and Limitations

The ongoing evaluation and assessment process was important in gaining an understanding of the immediate and long-term impacts of the Indicators of Engagement Project. Assessment is recognized as a critical tool that enables researchers to articulate what they are learning during the course of their work and to make incremental adjustments resulting in greater reliability of the data and methodology, leading to more valid findings (Gelmon, 2000). Assessment is especially useful in qualitative studies as theory and findings often emerge through the course of the work. This project, in particular, was conducive to a more reflective approach as the indicators were tested and refined as new knowledge emerged about the nature of civic engagement at community colleges. The evaluation component was therefore integrated throughout the entire project as part of a continuous cycle of learning through the steps of program development, delivery, and improvement. As a result, the evaluative component of this project enabled several timely modifications that improved strategies on behalf of the project goal.

All of the methodological instruments described were used to complete a comprehensive qualitative analysis of the site visit reports to determine the extent to which the indicators of engagement were observed. While the variety of methods employed ensured that a quality and reliable analysis was produced, some limitations should be kept in mind in interpreting the findings. These include: a) variability in style and approach among multiple site visitors; b) limited time on site visits, which may have restricted the scope of information collected; c) the limited number of responses to the initial survey; and d) the ability to generalize from a small number of observations.

Projects with multiple site visitors face concerns that each individual site visitor might use a standardized protocol quite differently, with some following it very attentively and others using it as a general guide but letting the conversation in each interview flow in a less structured way. The project team addressed this concern in several ways. First, the evaluators encouraged a single approach to interviewing to ensure that the site visitors obtained responses to all questions, regardless of the specific approach they used to get that information. In addition, an independent observer from the project team attended the first site visit with each visitor to observe and document interview procedures and recommend steps to standardize the approach among all three site visitors.

This normal variation among site visitors was also observed in the assessment of exemplars at the campuses they visited. What one person deems exemplary may be considered ordinary by another individual. This was addressed through multiple conversations and exchanges of documentation among the project team.

Another challenge was posed by scheduling constraints, since only one day on campus was available for each site visit. In some cases, not all questions related to a particular indicator were asked and, to a lesser degree, some stakeholder groups and their corresponding questions were omitted entirely. In other cases, some key individuals were not available during the site visit despite best efforts. To overcome this limitation, some follow-up interviews were conducted by telephone with key individuals after the site visit.

There was also some concern about the limited number of responses to the initial survey. Although the survey process revealed many exemplary practices, it is possible that some examples were not identified and remain unknown. In the next phases of this project, staff are addressing possible causes of non-response, including difficulties in identifying the most appropriate individual on a campus to respond, reducing the burden of survey completion through design and format changes, and increasing awareness of the survey among the target respondent group.

Conclusion

This initial work evaluating the manifestations of the indicators of engagement has confirmed the value of these indicators in assessing the depth, impact, and sustainability of campus-based engagement efforts. It has also revealed some overlap in the definitions of some of the indicators, such as "faculty development" and "faculty roles and rewards." As is expected in any application in practice of a theoretical model, one learns from application and makes necessary modifications to enhance the utility of the model for further application. This process will be reported upon in the subsequent work of the Indicators of Engagement Project.

Appendix II: Campus Compact's "Indicators of Engagement" Self-Assessment Guide

Using the Indicators to Assess and Deepen Campus Engagement

The following questions seek to document civic and community engagement using the framework of the 13 "indicators of engagement" developed by Campus Compact. Taken together, these indicators compose the building blocks of an engaged campus. The "engaged campus" has been defined as having "an integrated approach to fostering students' citizenship skills through both educational and co-curricular programs and activities, and conscious modeling of good institutional citizenship through external partnerships and activities" (Thomas, 2000, p. 66). An engaged campus reflects full acceptance of the larger sense of institutional alignment that Ernest Boyer identified as "the scholarship of engagement"; namely, scholarship that "connect[s] the rich resources of the university to our most pressing social, civic, and ethical problems" (Boyer, 1996a).

The indicators are designed to help campuses both assess their current level of engagement and create strategies to deepen their work. They recognize that institutions utilize approaches to engagement best suited to their particular culture and priorities. It is unlikely that any one campus, however engaged, will exhibit all of the indicators equally well. For this reason, the indicators are not prescriptive; their value lies primarily in the possibilities they suggest.

The questions below were adapted from the site visit protocol created for the first year of the Indicators of Engagement Project. During the site visits, Campus Compact scholars met with senior academic and administrative leaders, faculty, students, community partners, and the community service and/or service-learning director. We believe that these questions can provide valuable guidance for individuals wishing to assess civic and community engagement on their campus.

Recommended Procedure

Participants

The questions below are intended for a campus team consisting of senior academic and administrative leaders, faculty, students, community partners, and the community service and/or service-learning director.

First steps

We suggest that the campus designate a team (consisting of the stakeholders listed above) to guide the self-assessment based on the Indicators of Engagement. Once this team is in place, members should choose the indicators where the campus excels, and focus on those indicators and questions to begin the team's discussion.

Notes on Language

The questions have been written in a way to avoid "yes/no" answers. In almost all cases, you will want to ask participants to provide illustrations, descriptions, or examples so that you will have more detailed and complete answers.

We have attempted to avoid using the term "the community" as it is too sweeping, so in general we refer to community organizations or community partners. If it is situation-appropriate to use "the community," feel free to use this language instead.

As in any interview protocol, you may modify language as necessary to better communicate with the audience, so long as the core meaning of the question does not change. Since the questions reflect the detailed content of the indicators (included with each set of interview questions), please refer to this language in order to ensure any editorial changes do not affect the original intent of the indicators.

1. Mission and Purpose

Core Question: *How do civic engagement, service-learning, and related activities reflect the mission and purpose of the institution?*

Specific language of this indicator (for reference):

- The college's mission explicitly articulates its commitment to the public purposes of higher education and higher education's civic responsibility to educate for democratic participation.
- This aspect of the mission is openly valued and is explicitly used to promote and to explain the civic activities of the campus.
- The college demonstrates a genuine willingness to review, discuss, and strengthen the civic aspect of its mission.
- All campus constituencies demonstrate their familiarity with and ownership of the college's mission.

Questions:

1. Please describe the mission and purpose of the institution in your own words.
2. How is the mission publicized on campus and around the community (billboards, signs, logos, mottos on letterhead, etc.)?
3. Does the mission reflect civic and community engagement, service-learning, and/or community service? Please give some examples.
4. Does the mission statement provide the basis for establishing effective community-campus partnerships? How are you able to use your mission to support your community efforts?
5. Have you encountered resistance either within the college or from the community in general regarding the nature of your mission? How have you dealt with this resistance? Please give some examples.

➨ **Do these questions and the resulting conversation suggest any ways to better connect the institutional mission and purpose to your engagement efforts?**

Documentation to Review

Kinds of documentation/information you may wish to review include:

- Mission statement, plus statement of the institution's vision/values/purpose
- Promotional materials

- Institution homepage/website
- Membership in Campus Compact and/or leadership roles on Campus Compact's Board of Directors or Board committees
- President's corner on website
- Annual report
- Public paper trail of community development efforts (from public relations office)
- Publications by leaders—scholarly or op/ed on civic engagement/service-learning
- Examples of speeches by leaders—e.g., to board, legislators, or faculty—that reference the mission
- Media files

2. Administrative and Academic Leadership

Core Question: *How do academic and administrative leaders support civic engagement, service-learning, and related forms of experiential learning at the institution?*

Specific language of this indicator (for reference):

- The president, the chief academic officer, and the trustees visibly support campus civic engagement, in both their words and their actions.
- The president and the college's academic leaders have played a visible and committed role in helping the college evolve into a genuinely engaged institution.
- The campus is publicly regarded as an important and reliable partner in local community development efforts.

Questions:

1. In what ways do academic and administrative leaders promote civic and community engagement and related teaching/learning strategies both within the institution and to external communities?
2. What are some examples of the ways leaders demonstrate commitment to the community (public work by leaders, speeches, community involvement, support of community initiatives, participation on boards of community organizations, etc.)?
3. Are there formalized plans among institutional leaders regarding civic engagement practices? If so, please describe. Is there a strategic plan? Does it include civic or community engagement?
4. How is the commitment to engagement institutionalized? Would this continue if key leaders left the institution?
5. Does the institution use specific methods to assess the impact of its civic engagement activities? Please offer some examples. How do you use the results of these assessments?

Documentation to Review

Kinds of documentation/information you may wish to review include:

- Publications by leaders—scholarly or op/ed on civic engagement/service-learning
- Membership in Campus Compact and/or leadership roles on Campus Compact's Board of Directors or Board committees
- Examples of speeches by leaders—e.g., to board, legislators, or faculty—that support engagement

- President's corner on website
- Public paper trail of community development efforts (from public relations office)
- Institutional strategic plan

3. Disciplines, Departments, and Interdisciplinary Work

Core Question: *How is the commitment to civic engagement and community-based learning reflected in and across disciplines?*

Specific language of this indicator (for reference):

- Community-based learning opportunities can be found across the entire curriculum. It is as much the concern of the arts and humanities, the natural sciences, technical disciplines, pre-professional studies, and interdisciplinary programs as it is of the social sciences.
- Students have multiple opportunities to do community-based work in their general education and career (vocational, technical, occupational) curricula.
- Formal opportunities exist for capstone experiences (group reflection meetings, forums, variable credit courses, capstones often not credited by the university other than as elective credit) focused on community-based problems or issues in most disciplines.
- Academic units (i.e., departments and programs) rather than individual faculty members have assumed ownership of partnering activities.
- Course-based community initiatives are structured and/or coordinated across disciplines, such as learning communities, cohort and peer approaches, and thematically linked courses across semesters.

Questions:

1. How is the commitment to civic engagement and community-based learning reflected in and across disciplines?

2. Think about a department/discipline/program where the commitment to civic engagement is particularly strong. Please describe what contributes to this strength, and how this might be further developed or enhanced.

3. Think about a department/discipline/program where the commitment to civic engagement is minimal or nonexistent. Please describe what contributes to this lack of involvement, and how a commitment to civic engagement might be encouraged and initiated.

4. Have you encountered resistance from departments regarding the implementation of service-learning, community-based experiences, or other civic engagement activities? How have you dealt with this resistance (please give some examples)?

5. Are there opportunities to promote best practices in civic engagement and/or to share these activities with other departments and programs at the

college? *Probe for departmentally based activities, individual faculty development, other kinds of initiatives and learning opportunities.*

6. Are there specific opportunities or structures for interdisciplinary collaborations in community-based learning? If so, please give some examples. If not, are there any opportunities at the institution that could facilitate the development of interdisciplinary community-based collaborations?

Documentation to Review

Kinds of documentation/information you may wish to review include:

- Departmental promotional materials
- Department/program homepage/website
- Annual report (institution and/or departments)
- Public paper trail of community development efforts (from public relations office)
- Presentations and publications of faculty
- Documentation from office of community-based learning or volunteerism
- Community partner documentation on partnerships
- Samples of student projects from community-based classes

4. Pedagogy and Epistemology

Core Question: *How are the multiple sources of knowledge and contributions of instructors valued, incorporated, and acknowledged at the college?*

Specific language of this indicator (for reference):

- Community-based work provides an opportunity for students to generate knowledge, develop critical thinking skills, and grapple with the ambiguity of social problems.
- Community knowledge and community expertise are valued as essential to the education of engaged citizens and are incorporated in various ways throughout the curriculum.
- Experiential learning is valued both by faculty and by administrators as an academically credible method of creating meaning and understanding.
- High-level administrators include service-learning in their strategic plans for enhanced academic learning.
- Students are formally introduced to the concepts and skills necessary for community-based work early on in their academic careers.

Questions:

1. What role do campus leaders and faculty play in supporting the multiple approaches to teaching and learning that reflect the college's civic engagement commitment? What role do others play?
2. Have you encountered resistance either within the college or from the community in general regarding the implementation of service-learning, community-based experiences, or other civic engagement activities? How have you dealt with this resistance (please give some examples)?
3. How are community sources of knowledge valued, incorporated, and acknowledged at the college? Please give some specific examples of community involvement in course design/delivery, participation on college committees, and other activities.

Documentation to Review

Kinds of documentation/information you may wish to review include:

- Departmental promotional materials
- Department/program homepage/website
- Faculty presentations and publications

- Documentation of teaching innovations
- Formal agreements with partners
- Inventory/report of partnership activity
- Examples of syllabi
- Community partner documentation on campus partnership
- Samples of student projects from community-based classes
- Accreditation self study reports and documents

5. Faculty Development

Core Question: *What resources are available to faculty members (full-time, part-time, and adjunct instructors) to enhance their efforts?*

Specific language of this indicator (for reference):

- The college regularly provides faculty with in-house opportunities to become familiar with teaching methods and practices related to service-learning.
- Mechanisms have been developed to help faculty mentor and support each other in learning to design and implement service-learning courses.
- To enhance their ability to offer quality service-learning courses, faculty have access to curriculum development grants, reductions in teaching loads, and/or travel grants to attend regional and national conferences focused on engaged work.

Questions:

1. What kinds of faculty development activities does the college design, promote and provide? What has been the response of faculty to these activities? What are the results of the evaluations of these activities?

2. How does the college determine the needs of faculty for specific kinds of knowledge and skill development related to civic engagement, service-learning, and related strategies? Please describe the process. Once you get the results of these determinations, what do you do with the information? Who is responsible for translating these results into concrete development activities? *Please be sure to highlight central college functions vs. individual departmental functions.*

3. Without naming it, think about a department/discipline/program where the commitment to civic engagement is minimal or nonexistent. What is it about the faculty in this unit (based upon discipline, experience, etc.) that has kept them from developing such a commitment? What opportunities have you tried to provide to encourage them to develop knowledge and skills regarding civic engagement?

4. How are faculty prepared for the process of identifying suitable community partners? What support does the college provide? What other faculty development activities exist that specifically address how to orient partners to the expectations of community-based learning opportunities; how to involve them in the design of these experiences; how to determine appropriate roles for partners in assessment of student learning; and/or how to seek partners' evaluation of the overall experience?

5. How do programs/departments identify community partners for service-learning experiences? In general, are these partners suitable for these courses? Are the partners able to provide the support students need to complete their learning experience? Do the partners appear to understand what the expectations are in order for students to successfully complete both the community-based learning experience and the course?

Documentation to Review

Kinds of documentation/information you may wish to review include:

- Report(s) of faculty development unit (or similar center)
- Announcements of faculty development activities
- Evaluations of faculty development activities
- Lists of faculty attending various development activities
- Participation in Campus Compact training or other activities
- Other resources relevant to faculty development

6. Faculty Roles and Rewards

Core Question: *What are the specific ways the college demonstrates the importance of civic engagement with regard to roles and rewards for faculty (full-time, part-time and adjunct)?*

Specific language of this indicator (for reference):

- The college's tenure, promotion, and/or retention guidelines reflect a range of scholarly activities such as those proposed by Ernest Boyer (1990) in *Scholarship Reconsidered: Priorities of the Professoriate.*
- Faculty data forms, annual reports, and mandatory evaluations all include sections related to civic engagement, professional service, and/or other forms of academically based public work.
- The college explicitly encourages academic departments to include community-based interests and experience as criteria in their faculty recruiting efforts.

Questions:

1. Does the college have policies that support and reward faculty for civic engagement and related teaching and learning strategies (such as service-learning)? Please give some examples.

2. How are these policies publicized? How aware are faculty of these policies? How aware are students and community partners of these policies?

3. Does the college explicitly encourage academic departments to seek faculty with community-based interests and experience when they are recruiting new faculty? If so, please give some examples of how successful this strategy has been.

4. How do your policies regarding faculty participation in civic engagement relate to the overall college mission, goals, and strategic plans? Do these policies vary for full-time and adjunct faculty; if so, how?

5. In your opinion, is the College's commitment to recognizing and rewarding faculty for civic engagement and related activities something that can be sustained? Could it be replicated elsewhere, and if so, how? Does this recognition vary for full-time and adjunct faculty; if so, how?

Documentation to Review

Kinds of documentation/information you may wish to review include:

- Promotion and tenure guidelines
- Recruitment materials for new faculty

- Job descriptions for recent faculty searches
- Reports on community-based scholarship, presentations, research
- Numbers of individuals tenured/promoted based on civic engagement
- Utilization of resources such as the National Review Board on the Scholarship of Engagement

7. Enabling Mechanisms

Core Question: *What are the sources of tangible evidence of the college's commitment to promoting and sustaining civic engagement and related community-based learning strategies?*

Specific language of this indicator (for reference):

- The college maintains a centralized office that is committed to community-based teaching and learning and clearly aligned with academic affairs.
- The college has developed a full range of forms and procedures that allow it to organize and document community-based work.
- Faculty and students are kept well informed of the resources available to support community-based work. These resources are effectively included in all faculty and student orientation programs.
- The college recognizes the unusual demands created by work in the community and attempts to provide flexible scheduling options for faculty and students.
- The college recognizes that course content can be delivered in many ways and allows faculty sufficient freedom to utilize community-based strategies.
- The college recruits and trains student leaders to work with faculty and community partners.

Questions:

1. Do you have a centralized office that supports civic engagement (such as an office of service-learning, community service, or community partnerships)? If so, what is the role of this office? How long has it been in existence? What sorts of resources (staff, budget, physical space, etc.) support it? Are these sufficient? How does it facilitate integration of various civic engagement-related efforts? How does this office work with other college offices such as Student Affairs, Academic Affairs, or Volunteer Services?

2. What mechanisms exist to organize, document, and describe the multiple civic engagement activities in which the college is engaged? Please offer some specific examples. How well do these mechanisms work? How could they be improved, and to what end? Are course-based civic engagement activities integrated with other outreach activities? Please give some illustrations.

3. How are new faculty and students made aware of the college's commitment to promoting and sustaining civic engagement and related community-based learning strategies? What kinds of information are provided about specific policies, resources, and services?

4. How does the college accommodate the flexibility necessary to develop and deliver effective community-based learning experiences? Please give examples relevant both to faculty and to students (e.g., time commitments, scheduling, logistics, alternative course delivery strategies, etc.).

5. How does the college facilitate communication among faculty, academic units, college leaders, and community partners?

6. Given the various methods the college uses to facilitate civic engagement activities, do you think this commitment is sustainable? Why or why not? If not, what do you believe would be necessary to make it sustainable?

Documentation to Review

Kinds of documentation/information you may wish to review include:

- Center mission statement, website, annual report, activities report
- Faculty handbook
- Student handbook
- Schedules and supporting materials from faculty and student orientations
- Academic catalog
- Campus publications (reports to community, etc.)
- Media files
- Inventories of community partnerships, community-based activities
- Database summaries of community partners
- Presence/activities of community advisory boards
- Web-based resources

8. Internal Resource Allocation

Core Question: *What are the policies and practices regarding the internal allocation and stability of resources (including funding, staffing, and space) to support engagement activities?*

Specific language of this indicator (for reference):

- Adequate funding is provided to support, enhance, and deepen involvement by faculty, students, and staff in community-based work.
- The college regularly draws upon already existing resources to strengthen engagement activities. Such activities are seen as priorities in the allocation of those resources.
- The college provides sufficient long-term staffing for all core partnerships and engagement activities. It also provides adequate office space for that staff to do its work.

Questions:

1. What policies does the college have in place regarding the allocation of resources to promote and sustain civic engagement and related teaching/learning strategies? Who is responsible for allocating these resources (i.e., how are the policies put into practice)? Please give concrete examples related to fiscal, human, physical, information, technological, and/or other kinds of resources.

2. How are priorities established for the allocation of resources to support civic engagement activities? What formal positions, committees, or structures have responsibility for setting and communicating priorities? How effective are these in practice?

3. What mechanisms exist to organize, document, and describe the multiple civic engagement activities in which the college is engaged? Please give specific examples. How well do these mechanisms work? How could they be improved, and to what end?

4. Are any resources available to students, faculty or community partners to offset personal expenses for community-based work (such as costs related to transportation, background checks, etc.)? How do people find out about these resources? Are the resources available sufficient? If not, what other kinds of resources are needed?

Documentation to Review

Kinds of documentation/information you may wish to review include:

- Annual report, activities report
- Budget summary statements
- Budget guidelines; other policies on resource allocation
- President's priority funding list
- Campus publications (reports to community, etc.)
- Inventories of community partnerships, community-based activities
- Web-based resources, listservs, other information about community resources

9. Community Voice

Core Question: *How do community organizations participate in shaping the college's commitment to promoting and sustaining civic engagement and related community-based learning strategies?*

Specific language of this indicator (for reference):

- Community partners are deeply and regularly involved in determining their role in and contribution to community-based learning.
- Community partners play a significant role in helping shape institutional involvement in the community.
- Community partners are well represented on all relevant college-based committees.
- Community partners provide feedback on the development and maintenance of engagement programs and are involved in all relevant strategic planning.
- The college allocates resources to compensate community partners for their participation in service-learning courses.

Questions:

1. How does the college facilitate communication between the institution and its community partners? What mechanisms work particularly well to involve the community with the institution?

2. To what extent are community partners represented on relevant college committees? How are the representatives selected? What are their roles on various committees? *Probe for voting status, leadership roles, other decision-making responsibilities.*

3. Do community partners participate in the design of community-based courses? If so, what is their role? Do they participate in assessment of their involvement in courses, committees, and other activities? Are there opportunities for community partners to play more substantial roles in design, delivery, and evaluation of the college's various civic engagement activities?

4. What role do community representatives play in shaping the institution's involvement in community activities? Are community representatives involved in helping the institution to seek external funding for community-based activities? If so, how?

Documentation to Review

Kinds of documentation/information you may wish to review include:

- Annual report, activities reports
- Schedules and supporting materials from faculty and student orientations
- Academic catalog
- Agreements/contracts for community organization participation
- Campus publications (reports to community, etc.)
- Media files
- Inventories of community partnerships, community-based activities
- Presence/activities of community advisory boards
- Committee descriptions, membership listings, records as appropriate
- Web-based resources

10. External Resource Allocation

Core Question: *What are the policies and practices regarding the allocation and stability of resources (including funding, staffing, and space) externally to support engagement activities?*

Specific language of this indicator (for reference):

- The college helps community partners create a richer learning environment for students working in the community and assists them in accessing human, technical, and intellectual resources on campus.
- The college makes resources available for community-building efforts in local neighborhoods.
- Campus mechanisms have been designed and developed to serve both the campus and the local community (e.g., shared-use buildings).
- The college has intentionally developed purchasing and hiring policies that favor local residents and businesses.

Questions:

1. What policies does the college have in place that fund community partners in order to create a richer learning environment for students working in the community and to assist those partners in accessing human and intellectual resources on campus? Are resources made available for community-building efforts in local neighborhoods? Who is responsible for the allocation of these resources (i.e., how are the policies put into practice)? Please give some concrete examples related to fiscal, human, physical, information, technological, and/or other kinds of resources.

2. What specific resources exist that are examples of external resource allocation? For example, has the college developed purchasing and hiring policies that favor local residents and businesses? Or does it offer shared-use facilities or services (e.g., libraries, health facilities)? Please give some examples.

3. How are priorities established for external allocation of resources to support civic engagement–related activities? What formal positions, committees, or structures have responsibility for setting and communicating priorities? How effective are these in practice?

4. Are there any specific examples of situations where the college has made resources available to community organizations that would otherwise have not been affordable or available to them (e.g., library privileges, donations of

used computers, parking privileges, professional development courses, technical assistance such as in grant writing)? How did these situations come about? Were there formal or informal mechanisms that provided the community organizations with these special resources?

5. Do community partners receive any kind of compensation or other resources in recognition of their contribution to college activities? Please give some examples.

6. How do college leaders, faculty, and/or students participate in or contribute to community-building efforts? Please describe some examples.

Documentation Reviewed

Kinds of documentation/information you may wish to review include:

- Annual report, activities reports
- Budget summary statements
- Budget guidelines, other policies on resource allocation
- President's priority funding list
- Campus publications (reports to community, etc.)
- Community partner publications (annual reports, etc.)
- Inventories of community partnerships, community-based activities
- Web-based resources, listservs, other information about community resources

11. Integrated and Complementary Engagement Activities

Core Question: *How are the college's efforts regarding civic engagement integrated across the campus and with the community?*

Specific language of this indicator (for reference):

- The college effectively coordinates engagement and service-related activities across academic, co-curricular, and non-academic programs.
- The college makes it possible for community partners to understand, access, and easily navigate the full range of its engagement activities.

Questions:

1. In what ways do you integrate civic engagement and related teaching/learning strategies both within the college and with external communities? Please give some examples.
2. Do you have a centralized office that supports civic engagement (such as an office of service-learning, community service, or community partnerships)? If so, what is the role of this office? How does it facilitate integration of various civic engagement-related efforts? Do you anticipate the office will continue to exist in the future?
3. What roles do other college offices such as Student Affairs or Academic Affairs play in this integration? Please give some examples.
4. Are course-based civic engagement activities integrated with other community service and volunteer activities? Please give some illustrations.

Documentation to Review

Kinds of documentation/information you may wish to review include:

- Campus calendar of events
- Academic catalog
- Campus publications (reports to community, etc.)
- Inventories of community partnerships, community-based activities
- Database summaries of community partners
- Presence/activities of community advisory boards
- Web-based resources

12. Forums for Fostering Public Dialogue

Core Question: *What does the college do to foster public dialogue and raise awareness about its commitment to civic engagement?*

Specific language of this indicator (for reference):

- The college plays a visible and effective role in facilitating dialogue around important public issues.
- The college helps to bring together stakeholders from all sectors of the community.

Questions:

1. How does the college bring together various stakeholder groups to exchange information and participate in collective problem-solving regarding important public issues? In what ways does the college foster public dialogue in order to promote and sustain civic engagement and related teaching/learning strategies? Please give some concrete examples.

2. What offices or positions at the college are responsible for facilitating public dialogue? Please give some examples and describe specific roles. *Probe for centralized office, senior administrator, community outreach coordinator, lobbyist, etc.*

3. How does the college facilitate communications among internal and external stakeholders? What specific communication strategies and mechanisms are used regularly?

4. How do students and faculty know where to go on campus to become involved in issues pertinent to the community? What mechanisms exist to inform students and faculty? How do students and faculty gain additional information about college activities in community development and outreach?

5. How do community organizations know where to go on campus to seek college involvement in issues pertinent to the community? How do community organizations gain additional information about college activities in community development and outreach?

Documentation to Review

Kinds of documentation/information you may wish to review include:

- Annual report, activities reports
- Academic catalog
- Campus publications (reports to community, etc.)
- Media files
- Inventories of community partnerships, community-based activities
- Presence/activities of community advisory boards
- Documentation regarding student and faculty organizations
- Committee descriptions, membership listings, records as appropriate
- Web-based resources

13. Student Voice

Core Question: *How do students participate in shaping the college's commitment to promoting and sustaining civic engagement and related community-based learning strategies?*

Specific language of this indicator (for reference):

- Students participate on major institutional committees including those that make personnel decisions.
- The college recognizes student-initiated advocacy campaigns as legitimate forms of democratic practice.

Questions:

1. In student orientation programs, how are students made aware of the college's commitment to promoting and sustaining civic engagement and related community-based learning strategies? What kinds of information are provided about specific policies, resources and services? What roles do community organizations play in these orientations?

2. Do students participate in the design of community-based courses? If so, how? How do they participate in assessment of their involvement in courses, committees, and other activities? Are there opportunities for students to play more substantial roles in design, delivery, and evaluation of the college's civic engagement activities?

3. Are there official student organizations and/or committees at the college? What roles do these organizations and/or their leaders play in shaping the college's commitment to civic engagement? Please give some examples.

4. To what extent are students represented on college committees relevant to civic engagement? How are the representatives selected? What are their roles on various committees? *Probe for voting status, leadership roles, other decision-making responsibilities.*

5. What support does the college provide for student-initiated efforts with community organizations?

Documentation to Review

Kinds of documentation/information you may wish to review include:

- Annual report, activities reports
- Schedules and supporting materials from faculty and student orientations
- Academic catalog
- Campus publications (reports to community, etc.)
- Media files
- Inventories of community partnerships, community-based activities
- Presence/activities of community advisory boards
- Documentation regarding student organizations
- Committee descriptions, membership listings, records as appropriate
- Web-based resources

Appendix III: Key Campus Contacts for Colleges in This Study

Rudy M. Garcia
Director of Experiential Learning
Albuquerque Technical Vocational Institute
525 Buena Vista SE
Albuquerque, NM 87106
Phone: (505) 224-3068
Fax: (505) 224-3268
Email: rudyg@tvi.edu

Cathleen H. Doyle
Program Coordinator, Center for Learning Through Service
Anne Arundel Community College
101 College Parkway
Arnold, MD 21012
Phone: (410) 777-2902
Fax: (410) 777-4902
Email: chdoyle@aacc.edu

Roger Henry
Director, Center for Service-Learning
Brevard Community College
3865 N. Wickham Road
Melbourne, FL 32935
Phone: (321) 433-5610
Fax: (321)433-5649
Email: HenryR@brevardcc.edu

Chris Schnick
English Instructor
Chandler-Gilbert Community College
2626 East Pecos Road
Chandler, AZ 85225
Phone: (480) 732-7186
Email: chris.schnick@cgcmail.maricopa.edu

Terri Berryman
Director of Career and Placement Services
College of Lake County
19351 W. Washington St.
Grayslake, IL 60030
Phone: (847) 543-2059
Fax: (847) 543-2667 fax
Email: tberryman@clcillinois.edu

Regina M. Hughes
Director, Center for Scholarly and Civic Engagement
Collin County Community College District
Central Park Campus
2200 W. University
McKinney, TX 75071
Phone: (972) 548-6739
Email: rhughes@ccccd.edu

Elaine Dabelko
Associate Vice President of Special Projects
Hocking College
3301 Hocking Parkway
Nelsonville, OH 45764
Email: dabelko_e@hocking.edu

Marcia Shideler
Coordinator, Community-Based Learning
Johnson County Community College
12345 College Blvd.
Overland Park, KS 66210
Phone: (913) 469-8500, ext. 3570
Email: shideler@jccc.net

Louise Pagotto
Interim Assistant Dean of Arts & Sciences and Curriculum Management
Kapi'olani Community College
4303 Diamond Head Road
Honolulu, HI 96816
Phone: (808) 734-9517
Fax: (808) 734-9828

Nicholas Holton
Service-Learning Coordinator
Kirtland Community College
10775 North St. Helen Road
Roscommon, MI. 48653
Phone: (989) 275-5000 ext. 412
Fax: (989) 275-8745
Email: holtonn@k2.kirtland.cc.mi.us

Cecile Regner
Vice President for Faculty & Instruction
Malcolm X College
1900 W. Van Buren Street
Chicago, IL 60612
Phone: (312) 850-7048
Email: cregner@ccc.edu

Josh Young
Director, Center for Community Involvement
Miami Dade College
300 NE 2nd Avenue
Miami, FL 33132
Phone: (305) 237-7477
Fax: (305) 237-7580
Email: jyoung@mdc.edu

Sheri Denk
Coordinator, Service-Learning Program
Middlesex Community College
Service Learning
33 Kearney Square
Lowell, MA 01852
Phone: (978) 656-3159
Fax: (978) 656-3150
Email: denks@middlesex.mass.edu

Lea Ann Erickson
Director of Community Relations
Mount Wachusett Community College
444 Green Street
Gardner, MA 01440
Phone: (978) 630-9322
Email: lerickson@mwcc.mass.edu

Kim Smith, Ph.D.
Service-Learning Faculty Coordinator
Department of Sociology
Portland Community College
Sylvania, SS 217
PO Box 19000
Portland, OR 97280-0990
Phone: (503) 977-4097
Fax: (503) 977-4959

Lori Moog
Program Manager of Community Outreach
Raritan Valley Community College
P.O. Box 3300
Somerville, NJ 08876
Phone: (908) 526-1200 ext. 8284
Email: lmoog@raritanval.edu

Linda Gabrielson
Southern Maine Community College
2 Fort Road
South Portland, ME 04106
Phone: (207) 741-5606
Email: lgabrielson@smccme.edu

Marlene Cousens, M.A.
Reading Instructor/Tutor Coordinator
Education Department
Yakima Valley Community College
Yakima, WA 98907
Phone: (509) 574-4997
Email: mcousens@yvcc.cc.wa.us

A complete list of service/service-learning program websites for these colleges can be found on page 55.

References

Association of American Colleges and Universities. (2002). *Greater expectations: A new vision for learning as a nation goes to college.* Washington, DC: AAC&U.

Astin, A., Vogelgesang, L., Ikeda, E., & Yee, J. (2000). *How service learning affects students.* Los Angeles: UCLA, Higher Education Research Institute.

Bailey, T. (2003, January). *Community colleges in the 21st century: Challenges and opportunities.* (CCRC Brief #15). New York: Community College Research Center.

Bailey, T., & Weininger, E. (2002, December). *Educating immigrants and native minorities in CUNY community colleges.* (CCRC Brief #13). New York: Community College Research Center.

Barr, R.B., & Tagg, J. (1995, November/December). A new paradigm for undergraduate education. *Change, 27*(6).

Boyer, E. (1990). *Scholarship reconsidered: Priorities of the professoriate.* Princeton, NJ: Carnegie Endowment for the Advancement of Teaching.

Boyer, E. (1996a). The scholarship of engagement. *Journal of Public Service and Outreach, 1*(1), 11-20.

Boyer, E.L. (1996b). Five priorities for quality schools. *Education Digest, 62*(1), 4–5.

Breneman, D., & Nelson, S. (1981). *Financing community colleges: An economic perspective.* Washington, DC: The Brookings Institution.

Brint, S., & Karabel, J. (1991). *The diverted dream: Community colleges and the promise of educational opportunity in America, 1900–1985.* New York: Oxford University Press.

Calhoun, C. (1999). The changing character of colleges: Institutional transformations in American higher education. In B.A. Pescosolido & R. Aminzade (Eds.), *The social worlds of higher education.* Thousand Oaks, CA: Pine Forge Press.

Campus Compact (1999). *Building the service-learning pyramid.* Providence, RI: Campus Compact.

Campus Compact. (1999, 2004). *Presidents' declaration on the civic responsibility of higher education.* Providence, RI: Campus Compact. Available at www.compact.org/presidential/declaration.html.

Dewey, J. (1916). *Democracy and education.* New York: Macmillan.

Dubson, M. (Ed). (2001). *Ghosts in the classroom: Stories of college adjunct faculty—and the price we all pay.* Livingston, TX: T&T Publications.

Franco, R.W. (2000). *The community college conscience: Service-learning and training tomorrow's teachers.* (ECS Issue Paper). Denver, CO: Education Commission of the States.

Franco, R.W. (2002a). The civic role of community colleges: Preparing students for the work of democracy. *The Journal of Public Affairs,* VI (suppl. 1), 119–138.

Franco, R.W. (2002b). Our communities' colleges: Cultivating civic roots in a diverse democracy. In Larson-Keagy, E. (Ed.), *Through whose eyes: Service-learning and civic engagement from culturally diverse perspectives.* Mesa, AZ: Community College National Center for Community Engagement.

Furco, A. (2001). *Self-assessment rubric for the institutionalization of service-learning in higher education.* Providence, RI: Campus Compact.

Gappa, J., & Leslie, D. (1993). *The invisible faculty.* San Francisco: Jossey-Bass.

Gelmon, S.B. (2000, Fall). Challenges in assessing service-learning. *Michigan Journal of Community Service Learning* (Special Issue: Strategic Directions for Service Learning Research), 84-90.

Gelmon, S.B., Holland, B.A., Driscoll, A., Spring, A., & Kerrigan, S. (2001). *Assessing service-learning and civic engagement: Principles and techniques.* Providence, RI: Campus Compact.

Gladieux, L.E., & Swail, W.S. (1998). Postsecondary education: Student success, not just access. In S. Halpern (Ed.), *The forgotten half revisited: American youth and young families, 1988–2008.* Washington, DC: American Youth Policy Forum.

Gleazer, E.J. (1994). Foreword, in A.A. Witt et al. (Eds.), *America's community colleges: The first century.* Washington, DC: Community College Press.

Gottlieb, K., & Robinson, G. (2002). *A practical guide for integrating civic responsibility into the curriculum.* Washington, DC: Community College Press.

Hebel, S. (2003). California's budget woes lead colleges to limit access. *Chronicle of Higher Education, 50*(7), A21.

Henry, R. (1998). Community college and service-learning: A natural at Brevard Community College. In Zlotkowski, E. (Ed.), *Successful service-learning programs: New models of excellence in higher education.* Bolton, MA: Anker Publishing.

Hollander, E., & Saltmarsh, J. (2000, July/August). The engaged university. *Academe: Bulletin of the American Association of University Professors, 86*(4), 29–31.

Hollander, E., Saltmarsh, J., & Zlotkowski, E. (2001). Indicators of engagement. In Simon, L.A., Kenny, M., Brabeck, K., & Lerner, R.M. (Eds.). *Learning to serve: Promoting civil society through service-learning.* Norwell, MA: Kluwer Academic Publishers.

The Institute of Politics. (2000, Summer). Attitudes toward politics and public service: A national survey of college and university undergraduates. *Harvard Political Review.* Available at www.hpronline.org/survey.

Marchese, T. (1996, March). The search for next-century learning. *AAHE Bulletin, 3,* 3–6.

The Mellman Group. (2000). *Summary of national survey of 800 college students by the Mellman Group.* Seaside, CA: The Panetta Institute. Available at www.panettainstitute.org/poll~memo.htm.

Miller, M.A. (2003, March/April). Our students, ourselves. *Change, 35*(2), 4.

Morse, G.C. (2003). Virginia's community colleges: Ready, willing, but not enabled. *The Washington Post,* August 10, B08.

Musil, C.M. (2003). Educating for citizenship. *Peer Review, 5*(3), 5.

National Association of Secretaries of State. (1999). *New Millennium Project–Part 1: American youth attitudes on politics, citizenship, government and voting: Survey on youth attitudes.* Lexington, KY: National Association of Secretaries of State.

National Center for Education Statistics. (2000). *National assessment of educational progress.* Washington, DC: U.S. Department of Education.

The National Commission on Civic Renewal. (1998). *A nation of spectators: How civic disengagement weakens America and what we can do about it.* College Park, MD: The National Commission on Civic Renewal.

Phillippe, K.A., & Patton, M. (2000). *National profile of community colleges: Trends and statistics.* Washington, DC: Community College Press.

Prentice, M., Exley, B., & Robinson, G. (2003). *Sustaining service-learning: The role of the chief academic officer.* Project Brief. Washington, DC: Community College Press.

Prentice, M., Robinson, G., & McPhee, S. (2003). *Service-learning in community colleges: 2003 national survey results.* Washington, DC: Community College Press. Available at www.aacc.nche.edu.

President's Commission on Higher Education. (1947). *Higher education for American democracy.* Vol. 1, 69–70.

Sax, L.J., Astin, A.W., Korn, W.S., & Mahoney, K.M. (1999). *The American freshman: National norms for fall 1999.* Los Angeles: Higher Education Research Institute.

Schroeder, C. (1993, September/October). New students—new learning styles. *Change 25*(5), 21–26.

Sullivan, W. (1999). *The university as citizen: Institutional identity and social responsibility.* Washington, DC: The Council on Public Policy Education.

Thomas, N. (2000). The college and university as citizen. In T. Ehrlich (Ed.), *Civic responsibility and higher education.* Phoenix, AZ: ORYX Press.

Trounstine, J. (2001). *Shakespeare behind bars: The power of drama in a women's prison.* New York: St. Martin's Press.

Walshock, M. (1995). *Knowledge without boundaries: What America's research universities can do for the economy, the workplace, and the community.* San Francisco: Jossey-Bass.